CORPORATE PROFITABILITY & LOGISTICS INNOVATIVE GUIDELINES FOR EXECUTIVES

BY
ERNST & WHINNEY
NATIONAL DISTRIBUTION/LOGISTICS GROUP

FOR THE
COUNCIL OF LOGISTICS MANAGEMENT
AND
NATIONAL ASSOCIATION OF ACCOUNTANTS

This report prepared under contract to

The Council of Logistics Management

2803 Butterfield Road #380

Oak Brook, Illinois 60521 (312) 574-0985

and

The National Association of Accountants

10 Paragon Avenue, P.O. Box 433

Montvale, New Jersey 07645 (201) 573-6211

By

Ernst & Whinney

National Distribution/Logistics Group

1225 Connecticut Avenue, N.W., Washington, D.C. 20036

(202) 862-6000

CONTENTS

ACKNOWLEDGMENTS

As is often the case with comprehensive books, several people deserve special thanks for their contributions to making this one meaningful and readable. First, for their patience and persistence, we acknowledge the executive director of the Council of Logistics Management (the Council)--George Gecowets--as well as the managing director of professional services of the National Association of Accountants (NAA)--Albert King. Since 1981, these individuals have joined forces to sponsor landmark studies on financial management of physical distribution. Their commitment has made possible three books on the subject. The first two focused on cost management techniques; this third one addresses the broader topic of corporate profitability. The persistence of Messrs. Gecowets and King accounts for the quality and usefulness of these publications.

The three books were produced under the direction of three different steering committees, and a name change for one of the sponsoring organizations (the Council was previously known as the National Council of Physical Distribution Management). The third steering committee, which guided the research for this text, deserves special mention because of its acceptance of a difficult challenge, and its diligence in pursuing the project. These committee members--industry experts in their own right--include:

Blaine Ross, Bristol-Myers Co. (Chairman)

Philip Alling, Ciba-Geigy Corporation

Judith Bielenberg, Union Pacific

Dennis Clardy, Nabisco Brands, Inc.

Michael Todres, J.C. Penney Co., Inc.

Charles Grant, Chilton Company

Albert King, NAA

Patrick Romano, NAA

Elaine Winter, Council of Logistics Management

Of these people, Phil Alling, Chuck Grant, and Elaine Winter have stayed with us throughout the five years, a fact we consider particularly commendable. Elaine was responsible for managing publication of all three reports. We extend special thanks for her effort and commitment.

In preparing this third book, we engaged Lisa Harrington as text editor. Lisa, a logistics writer for **Traffic Management** magazine, translated our technical drafts into readable language for the business community. Because she knows logistics, Lisa's interpretations were always on the mark.

Ernst & Whinney made possible our investment of time and effort during the five-year period. We appreciate the firm's support of and commitment to these projects. Our Manufacturing Committee and Transportation Industry Group were especially helpful in contributing insights derived from client relationships--be they accounting and auditing, management consulting, or tax counseling. Additionally, our National Distribution/Logistics Consulting Group staff were of invaluable assistance in contributing to and reviewing drafts. In particular, Harvey Shycon, our Director of Distribution Planning and Customer Service Consulting, contributed heavily to those sections on topics in which he has achieved national prominence. As usual, John Clem, our technical editor, managed the production process in outstanding fashion. Also, our profound thanks go to June Anderson who typed and retyped our many drafts.

The most important contributors to this five-year research, however, were our clients and friends in the firms that allowed us to study their operations. While we cannot credit all the executives in the 120 or so companies involved, we would like to thank the members of the third steering committee, who are listed above, as well as members of former steering committees. The latter group includes:

John Boros, PPG Industries, Inc.

James Childers, Garvey Industries

Robert Stevenson, Williamhouse-Regency, Inc.

Gary Conway, Southwire Company

Charles Harrison, Johnson & Johnson

Jerry L. Ford, Pillsbury Company

Dale Humphrey, Alcan Aluminum Corporation

Edward Scott, Bristol-Myers Company

Lastly, we would like to thank the four executives who participated in our presentation, "Corporate Profitability and Logistics," at the Council's 1986 Annual Conference in Anaheim, California. These individuals, who were kind enough to share their companies' logistics innovations with conference attendees, include: Gerald Bodrie, General Motors Corp.; John Matson, Johnson & Johnson; Michael Todres, J.C. Penney Co.; and Seymour Zivan, Xerox Corporation. (We discuss this panel session in Chapter 2, "Successful Logistics Operations.") Their work, and the efforts of all other innovative logistics and business professionals, continue to help advance awareness of the increasingly important value of logistics to U.S. industry.

John R. Busher

and

Gene R. Tyndall

ERNST & WHINNEY

National Distribution

and Logistics Group

PREFACE

The information on which this report is based was collected during the five years that the Council and NAA sponsored the research. This information base was augmented by the many years of logistics experience of the authors, and the thousands of collective years of experience brought to bear by the many advisors we consulted.

In seeking out logistics excellence for this book, we investigated every lead possible in the nine months or so of research. In many cases, we refer to a practice or a program without mentioning the name of the company. We do this because it is policy at these firms to prohibit such disclosure. This request for anonymity is significant. It reflects management's realization that innovative logistics offers very real competitive advantage. In effect, these companies want to protect their new "secret weapon."

Like the authors of **In Search of Excellence**, we chose to distill this large data and information base into a set of findings--10 principles, to be exact. In studying these principles, we found that the intensity with which world-class companies execute them is a key contributor to their excellence and profitability. The executives we interviewed stated they wish their companies would achieve excellence in **all 10** areas. We believe these 10 principles represent "uncommon sense." They are practices that most executives regard as common sense, but overlook so often that they are not part of their companies' routines. Defining and elaborating on these principles of uncommon sense is the primary purpose of this book.

INTRODUCTION

The corporate activity known as logistics has undergone a quiet revolution during the past ten years. The fundamental nature of the discipline has changed, and so has the role that the logistics activity plays in the strategies of successful corporations.

Five years ago, when the Council of Logistics Management and the National Association of Accountants realized that the logistics activity was in transition, the two organizations established a joint research design and evaluation committee to study the nature and impact of this transition. At the recommendation of this joint committee, the two organizations contracted with Ernst & Whinney for a series of studies intended, first, to identify cost accounting and control techniques in transportation activities of the corporation; second, to identify cost accounting and control techniques in warehouse activities of the corporation; and third, to identify those management practices that have proved profitable in directing the logistics activities of the more successful corporations.

The first phase of this research was completed in 1983 with the publishing of the report, **Transportation Accounting and Control: Guidelines for Distribution and Financial Management.** The second phase was completed in 1985 when **Warehouse Accounting and Control: Guidelines for Distribution and Financial Managers** was published.

A combination of ongoing research and interviews with corporate executives caused us to broaden the perspective of the third study. We noticed that realizing logistics' potential contribution to corporate profitability requires much more than state-of-the-art financial controls. It demands a complement of integrated management practices which, for this third phase of the research, we identify and describe. These integrated management practices make up the very core of the relationship between corporate profitability and logistics.

Reducing the costs of producing and distributing products, while improving quality and service to customers, is a goal of most corporate executives. Tangible improvements in cost, quality, and service are critical in today's competitive markets. In fact, such improvements often determine a business unit's survival.

The sense of urgency brought on by this "survival of the fittest" environment is prompting more and more companies to examine, restructure, and re-position their operations to gain competitive advantage. Logistics, sometimes overlooked in this process, can be vital in implementing the integration and differentiation strategies designed to produce this advantage.

To explore logistics' impact on corporate profitability, we worked with senior logistics executives known for improving corporate profits through logistics decisions. We delved into how their business decisions impact profitability and add value to their companies' products and services.

Our research focuses on pinpointing exactly what principles determine the success of a logistics operation. Naturally, every logistics organization we study is unique in many respects. We find, however, that successful logistics organizations adhere to a handful of essential principles that transcend industry or company type.

These principles of logistics excellence, as we call them, are neither startling nor revolutionary; in fact, some consider them obvious or mundane. We think of them as "uncommon sense"; i.e., practices that most executives regard as common sense, but overlook so often that they are not part of their companies' routines.

Realistically speaking, even the best logistics operation is unlikely to impact a company as dramatically as, say, a major new product. Witness the effect the personal computer has had on profitability for computer giant IBM.

Logistics, however, can be a critical factor in ensuring the success of new products or other strategic initiatives. As testimony to this fact, the microcomputer industry boasts a graveyard filled with companies offering competitive products backed by fatally uncompetitive distribution/service operations.

Fortunately, this scenario occurs less and less frequently. Leading-edge companies now consider logistics strategies at the start of any new venture. General Motors executives, for example, focused on logistics issues in the preliminary stages of planning the company's new Saturn operation.

In fact, more and more senior executives now realize the importance of logistics to the success of their corporate strategies. In the companies studied for this project, we found that logistics excellence enables them to turn an activity traditionally considered a "service function" into a strategic resource contributing measurably to market share and profitability.

Myriad factors make a logistics operation "world class." Each company we worked with follows a different approach to making the most of logistics operations. Underlying these tactics, however, are 10 basic principles we identified as common to all excellent logistics departments. When taken together, these principles create the foundation for logistics excellence by allowing companies to achieve the function's full profit potential.

None of the executives with whom we worked are completely satisfied with the state of logistics development in his/her company. In every case, these individuals feel there are one or more principles needing additional attention. (That continual quest for improvement in itself is a characteristic that differentiates the "winners" from the other "players" in the logistics arena.)

The executives agreed, however, on the broad applicability of the 10 principles, and on their worth in understanding the formula for logistics success. Therefore, we adopted these 10 maxims as the framework for presenting our findings, and as guidelines for achieving and sustaining improved corporate profitability through logistics actions.

As our findings in this third study reveal, the logistics "winners" are those companies that implement the 10 principles of excellence on both a day-to-day and long-term basis. The payoff for their efforts is substantial. These companies boast smooth-running logistics operations; consistently high-quality, cost-effective customer service; participation in corporate strategy-making; and an overall improvement in logistics return on assets. That last item has the kind of direct impact on the corporate bottom line that makes chief executives sit up and take notice.

PART I: TODAY'S BUSINESS OF LOGISTICS

Chapter 1

THE ROLE OF LOGISTICS IN PROFITABLE COMPANIES

In the world of business, the functions of logistics, physical distribution, or materials management have been taken for granted for so long that we are pleasantly surprised when a senior executive recognizes their true value. Like marketing, manufacturing, or finance, logistics has its own society, its own terminology, and its own business purpose. The fact remains, however, that unlike marketing, manufacturing, or finance, logistics is not a household word. The purview of logistics seems different in every company, regardless of its products, services, or industry. And the titles associated with the function change so often that we find ourselves constantly asking logistics executives, "What do you do?"

Those of us involved in the profession have often been our own worst enemies, by changing our business terms so frequently. Fortunately we have allowed our basic purpose--getting the right product to the right place, at the right time, at the right cost, and in the right condition--to remain virtually unchanged.

Admittedly, this basic purpose still has relevance and value. Most companies would be delighted to achieve it fully every day. Modern logistics practice, however, has become much broader than this simple functional definition implies. In fact, more and more companies are reorganizing entire management teams in order to integrate the expanded logistics function comfortably into the organizational structure. Just what is logistics today? The new definition, adopted by the Council of Logistics Management and membership in 1985, provides a useful framework:

"...The definition of logistics is the process of planning, implementing, and controlling the efficient, cost-effective flow and storage of raw materials, in-process inventory, finished goods, and related information from point of origin to point of consumption for the purpose of conforming to customer requirements...."

As a working definition of logistics, this statement covers the pertinent characteristics of the discipline. It includes the "flow and storage" of items through the pipeline, from raw materials to customer delivery, and it builds on the need to "conform to customer requirements." Note that the definition also includes "information," a commodity that is becoming almost as valuable as finished products in terms of effective business management.

During our five years of studying logistics on behalf of the Associations, we have observed remarkable changes in the way American industry perceives individual functions. For example, partial deregulation of transportation in 1980 has created enormous changes in the structure of motor carriers, railroads, and airlines. These changes, in turn, have revolutionized the way in which manufacturing, merchandising, and distribution companies purchase transportation services. Moreover, heavy pressure to reduce costs has resulted in lower inventories and less warehousing. These variables are compounded by the fact that Japanese influence on efficiency and productivity has revised our thinking about partnerships with suppliers and customers.

With all these major changes occurring in industry, why has the perception of logistics in executive offices not evolved in concert? Continual changes in logistics terminology, we believe, have hampered such evolution. One intent of this book, therefore, is to help update the profession's image. Additionally, we designed the research to address the increasing number of questions by American business executives as to the distribution/logistics' potential for contributing to overall profitability. These questions are typified by the following comment from a CEO of a leading **Fortune** 200 company:

...I now know what physical distribution can do to save money. Tell me what it can do to improve my profits, to increase my share of the market, to improve my cash flow, to open new territories, to introduce new products, and to get the stockholders and board of directors off my back....

Notice that the chief executive asks if logistics can do anything important for profitability, and if so, what? Logistics must make this profitability contribution if it is to expand its role in the company.

THE VALUE CHAIN CONCEPT

We at Ernst & Whinney have been impressed over the past decade with the research into competitive strategy undertaken by Michael Porter of the Harvard Business School. In his first book, **Competitive Strategy**, Porter described three generic strategies for achieving competitive advantage: cost leadership, differentiation, and focus.[1] He also set forth a useful framework for analyzing industries and competitors in terms of these three strategies.

Porter's second book, published in 1985, generated major interest among planners and business managers in his methods and their applications. In **Competitive Advantage: Creating and Sustaining Superior Performance**, Porter went beyond the analysis framework to describe how a company can (and does) put the generic strategies into practice.[2] More specifically, he addresses questions such as: How does a firm gain a sustainable cost advantage? How can it differentiate itself from competitors? How does a company choose a market segment so that competitive advantage grows out of a focus-based strategy? When and how can a firm gain competitive advantage from competing with a coordinated strategy in related industries? How is uncertainty introduced into the pursuit of competitive advantage?

How can a firm defend its competitive position? Porter asserts that competitive advantage derives from the value a company creates for its buyers. This value may take the form of selling equivalent product at below-competitor prices. Or, value can manifest itself in the provision of unique benefits that offset a premium price. Porter uses a tool called "the value

3

chain" to separate buyers, suppliers, and a firm into the discrete but interrelated activities from which value stems. The value chain concept may be used to identify and understand the specific sources of competitive advantage, and how they relate to buyer value.

Published on the heels of the extraordinarily successful business book, **In Search of Excellence** by Tom Peters and Bob Waterman, Porter's text truly adds value to the state of business practice.[3] While Peters and Waterman so proficiently describe the innovations that make up successful American companies, Porter gives us an additional means of evaluating our own companies across the many disciplines or activities. In developing the value chain concept, Porter provides a systematic way of examining the activities a company performs and how they interact. The value chain is a concept, yes. However, it also is a proven and practical tool for determining how to **sustain** competitive advantage in an increasingly competitive marketplace.

Why does the value chain theory help us to determine the role of logistics in profitable companies? First of all, the concept recognizes how the logistics function fits into the business pipeline. In the diagram below, which we adapted slightly from Porter, note that logistics represents two of the five primary business activities that add value to a product (or service). We believe Porter is the first leading business scholar/practitioner to acknowledge this process and link it specifically to competitive advantage.

THE VALUE CHAIN

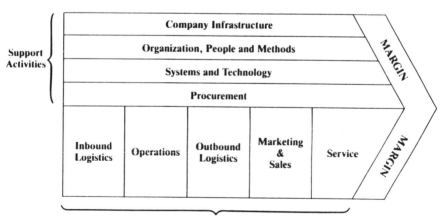

4

It is meaningful to review how Porter defines the five categories of primary activities involved in competing in any industry:

- **Inbound logistics.** Activities associated with receiving, storing, and disseminating inputs to the product, such as materials handling, warehousing, inventory control, vehicle scheduling, and returns to suppliers.

- **Operations.** Activities associated with transforming inputs into the final product form, such as machining, packaging, assembly, equipment maintenance, testing, printing, and facility operations.

- **Outbound logistics.** Activities associated with collecting, storing, and physically distributing the product to buyers, such as finished-goods distribution, warehousing, materials handling, delivery-vehicle operation, order processing, and scheduling.

- **Marketing and sales.** Activities associated with providing a means by which buyers can purchase the product and inducing them to do so, such as advertising, promotion, salesforce management, quoting, channel selection, channel relations, and pricing.

- **Service.** Activities associated with providing service to enhance or maintain the value of the product, such as installation, repair, training, parts supply, and product adjustment.

Note that the activities Porter lists under inbound and outbound logistics generally match the Council's definition of the discipline cited earlier. The information factor outlined by the Council is viewed by Porter (and by us) as a key support activity. Indeed, Porter has published articles on "information power" as a major source of competitive advantage.

While interviewing dozens of executives in leading corporations during the past several years, we looked for innovative activities within inbound or outbound logistics that create value and competitive advantage for those firms. The value chain concept provides a useful framework for seeking this information and positioning it within the business units. This is not necessarily because of the structure the value chain provides. Rather, it is the ability of the approach to detect and expose "linkages," or relationships between the way one value activity is performed, and the cost or performance of another.

For example, logistics managers have long been aware of the classic conflicts of interest that exist within all companies with respect to stock levels and customer service. Sales and marketing, in order to gain market share, push for high service and stock levels; production, to avoid disrupting factors, lobbies for higher stocks and lower service levels; finance and control, with tight budgets, argue for reduced stock. As managers of both service and stocks, logistics people are caught in the middle, trying to find and sustain the right balance of cost, inventories, and service.

The linkages exposed through value chain analysis reflect the "trade-offs" made among activities to achieve competitive advantage. They also reflect the need to coordinate different functions. On-time delivery, for example, a goal of most companies, requires coordination of activities in operations, outbound logistics, service, and sales/marketing. Because the same task can be accomplished in different ways, with different costs and performance, assessing activities and their linkages is crucial to understanding how logistics can impact corporate profitability.

The role of logistics in today's and tomorrow's profitable companies, then, will change as the value of products changes, and as the value that buyers or customers ascribe to products changes. This statement represents a new concept for many logistics managers, who were trained in transportation, warehousing, and other such functions to conduct their activities based on least-cost or other hard-measure priorities. To respond, therefore, to the CEO question we cited earlier, modern logistics managers must find innovative ways to help their companies improve profits, increase market share, improve cash flow, open new territories, introduce new products, and get the stockholders and board of directors "off the president's back." This is a major challenge for logistics managers, but one that is helped by the principles and examples in this book.

Chapter 2
SUCCESSFUL LOGISTICS OPERATIONS--THE PRINCIPLES INTRODUCED

Recognizing the role of logistics in profitable companies helps us understand how the function fits into the overall scheme of business. We must go beyond this recognition, however, to identify precisely what makes logistics operations successful.

A growing number of logistics managers have begun to ask themselves, "How are we doing?" and "How do we measure up against our key competitors?" For example, at one of the nation's largest diversified corporations, we have been working with customer-service executives in three areas: first, to define innovative ways of measuring performance; second, to use market intelligence to assess how their primary competitors are perceived by their customers; and third, to determine how the company can leverage its logistics strengths and correct its weaknesses to gain and sustain market share.

The activities at this company are typical of those occurring with increasing frequency at manufacturing, merchandising, and distribution organizations. Our research into what makes logistics a success in terms of corporate profitability shows that innovative companies continually assess their strengths and weaknesses, work closely with customers and suppliers, and challenge their measures of performance. Just as Tom Peters found in best-run companies, we discovered that excellent logistics operations are, above all, brilliant on the basics. They do not allow analysis to impede action. And, they persist and insist on top quality. In fact, Peters's eight attributes of excellence are present, in one form or another, in these logistics departments.

Our search for logistics excellence uncovered one critical factor that transcended all others--the value chain linkage we described above. Profitable logistics operations must be able to link their actions to marketing, production, corporate strategy, and other business functions. These linkages serve one major purpose--to keep the customer satisfied. Reflecting this philosophy, the best logistics managers describe their operations in the context of customers first; and other business activities second.

We would be remiss if we failed to mention a key factor not included in our 10 principles, but nonetheless critical to success. We refer to the existence of the corporate culture or philosophy.

Much has been written and discussed about this intangible, yet powerful, underlying factor of performance. When we assess the logistics operation, or any other value activity of the company, we must understand how this affects the way in which a firm operates and evolves. The successful logistics operations either became that way because of a culture that facilitates innovation and value linkages, or because their managers worked around or through the culture to achieve success. We do not describe in detail corporate culture or "politics" in this book. Nevertheless, we recognize its existence in all environments and its effects on the logistics principles of excellence.

We were very pleased to present a lively panel session at the Council of Logistics Management Annual Conference in 1986 on the topic, "Corporate Profitability and Logistics." Four leading logistics executives participated in the panel, helping us present our preliminary findings. These executives, all of whom manage unique, progressive logistics operations at their respective companies, included:

- **John Matson**, Director of Materials Management, Johnson & Johnson.

- **Gerald Bodrie**, Executive Director, Logistics Operations, General Motors.

- **Seymour Zivan**, Vice President, Logistics and Distribution, Xerox.

- **Michael Todres**, Vice President, Distribution, J.C. Penney Co., Inc.

The panelists described certain activities at their companies that illustrate the 10 principles of logistics excellence. We summarize these principles, and related remarks of the panelists, in the remainder of this chapter.

THE PRINCIPLES

#1-LINK LOGISTICS TO CORPORATE STRATEGY

All aspects of logistics operations must be directly linked to the corporate strategic plan. This is the first and most important rule in achieving the profit-improvement potential of logistics.

Many of the executives with whom we worked shared a common goal. They manage the logistics functions to support their company's strategy for achieving competitive advantage, be it through cost leadership, service differentiation, or both. These logistics heads operate under the premise that their department/division performs a value-added activity.

In managing their departments, these executives constantly ask, "Does our logistics operation make us more or less competitive in our key markets?" All too often, customers lament that they do business with a supplier despite its poor distribution performance. Such suppliers rely on superior products or marketing/sales efforts--not logistics service--to maintain market-share status quo.

Because of historical deficiencies in logistics, too many companies settle for a logistics operation that is a neutral element within the company. Top management in these firms views logistics as a "necessary evil." Unfortunately, this outdated attitude is present in all too many executive suites.

Pioneering logistics executives, however, have altered that view among their top management. They make certain the executive suite understands the true magnitude of costs controlled or influenced by logistics (more than

50 percent of sales in some companies). They also point up the significant bottom-line contributions generated by effective logistics-cost management.

In industries such as bulk commodities or automotives, where logistics represents a large percentage of total cost, an efficient, low-cost logistics operation is an important source of competitive advantage. Cost-effective logistics also impacts companies' standing in highly competitive areas such as consumer products, where even a small cost advantage is vital. For example, several grocery manufacturers give top priority to improving logistics productivity. Although their approaches differ, their objectives are similar: to effect major cost reductions that allow more competitive prices, add directly to the bottom line, or both.

One of the most popular approaches to gaining competitive advantage today is for firms to be the superior-service supplier in their markets. Recent emphasis on "getting close to customers" and striving for quality in all aspects of operations seems responsible for this trend.

One consumer-foods manufacturer, for example, uses a team of sales and distribution personnel to "sell" superior service in presentations tailored to individual customers' needs. The team highlights the specific customer-service measures and operations approaches they use to deliver the promised levels of service.

Related to cost leadership and service differentiation is logistics innovation. Some companies prefer to develop a new approach, rather than rely on being the best at performing the traditional one. Once these new approaches succeed, management uses them as a source of competitive advantage.

For instance, one consumer-goods manufacturer felt it had market logistics cost advantage in certain areas. The firm embarked on a multi-year program to popularize an approach to Direct Product Profitability (DPP) that emphasized the cost areas in which it excelled. Perseverance paid off. Today, the industry-standard DPP model favors their operations over those of competitors. This helps the company portray its products as the most profitable for retailers to carry.

#2-ORGANIZE COMPREHENSIVELY

The second principle of excellence calls for a comprehensive logistics organization that controls all corporate logistics functions under a single business unit. Materials management, transportation, warehousing, distribution, inbound logistics--whatever functions are relevant--should be unified under an appropriate mix of centralized and decentralized management.

Providing appropriate logistics service levels requires close coordination of operations with the business strategy. Low-cost logistics involves continual trade-offs (e.g., greater transportation spending for lower inventory and warehouse costs). Good decisions in both areas are easier to make if a single executive is responsible for all closely related logistics functions.

Despite the logic in grouping all logistics-related functions under a single umbrella, relatively few companies structure their activities in this manner. Industry has made progress toward this end during the past five years, but movement is gradual and evolutionary.

Encouragingly, we are beginning to see companies integrate two important areas--materials management and distribution. The search for better utilization of transportation and warehouse assets is responsible, in part, for this development. Companies' adoption of the "value chain" concept confirms the logic of such integration. These firms manage the entire logistics pipeline as a single, integrated flow using the complete range of supporting structures and assets available.

If logistics functions are unified under a single control, what mix of centralized and decentralized management works best? We find the best place to address the centralization/decentralization issue is at the activity level, rather than at the broader function level. Selecting the appropriate carrier for an individual shipment, for example, is a decision often best made at the field level. On the other hand, deciding issues of national scope is most effectively done by headquarters personnel.

Most companies that centralized distribution operations in the 1970s are decentralized today, reverting to more field-based logistics decision making. Increased use of computer-based systems, discussed below, has speeded this shift.

#3-USE THE POWER OF INFORMATION

Successful logistics departments take full advantage of information and information-processing technology. These departments view both transaction-based and decision-support systems as essential resources for realizing the profit potential of logistics. Electronic data interchange links with customers, for example, can be a source of competitive differentiation and increased market share. Creative use of computer-based models can yield cost/service improvements which also bolster competitive advantage.

Information is one of the few business resources that has declined markedly in cost over the last decade. As a result, companies increasingly consider investments in information-management systems as an alternative to expenditures for more conventional logistics assets. One manufacturer we studied reduced raw material inventory levels at a key plant from a four-day to a four-hour supply, largely by installing an improved data system linking manufacturing, logistics, suppliers, and carriers.

In the past, most computerized systems devoted to logistics focused on transaction processing (e.g., order processing, purchasing, inventory, etc.). This situation is changing rapidly. Many companies are developing versions of these systems that use the speed and expanded capabilities of the new generation computer and telecommunications hardware.

Some executives are looking beyond speed/capacity enhancements to systems that offer decision-support capabilities. During the next decade, these decision-support networks will evolve into "expert systems" that play major roles in logistics decision making.

A number of companies already use sophisticated computer models to aid in tactical and operational decision making. One such model analyzes specific product mixes in orders, and decides where to locate transportation equipment at the dock in order to minimize warehouse travel distances.

Experience has shown that system development and enhancement are most effective when conducted as an evolutionary--not revolutionary--process. The large database management complexities alone create growth problems. Many businesses now avoid the "big bang" approach to systems overhaul, whereby they implement a single, massive, multi-year project designed to meet the logistics information needs of the next decade. Logistics departments have been "burned" in the past by this "all-or-nothing" approach.

By developing "quick and dirty" systems prototypes (often in a microcomputer environment), a company can experiment with and refine new systems-development approaches. As a result, the firms can reap the benefits of the new application immediately.

One company we analyzed designed a microcomputer system to budget and control over $75 million in transportation costs. It recovered the system-development expense during the first quarter of use, and expects first-year savings to pay for the mainframe version of the software.

#4-EMPHASIZE HUMAN RESOURCES

Enlightened human-resource management is vital to achieving logistics excellence. In every case we examined, logistics excellence flourishes in an environment that recognizes people as the department's most important resource. Recruiting, education, training, and job enrichment are standard practice. Management acknowledges individuals for productivity gains, and in some cases, sets up incentive programs to foster excellence within the logistics function.

Senior logistics executives understand that experienced, well-trained managers are critical to the success of their strategies and plans. Today's logistics departments, however, demand a new breed of logistics manager. Finding these innovators can be a worrisome job for logistics-operations heads. One such executive at a major manufacturer told us he considers recruiting so critical that he and his chief assistants spend significant blocks of time meeting with professors and students.

In a related development, these same executives are increasingly concerned about their suppliers' human-resource management efforts. As more corporations form long-term strategic alliances with outside vendors, human-resource management becomes a shared concern. One logistics executive organized meetings between outside personnel experts and senior management at his company's key carriers to ensure these firms have adequate staff depth to provide stable operations.

In the training area, we found that management no longer views on-the-job training as a sufficient guarantee of a successful logistics operation. Many corporations send logistics managers and staff to formal training programs aimed at upgrading skills and introducing new concepts and techniques.

In some cases, such outside training is essential in subsequent implementation of new management approaches and systems. For example, one consumer-products manufacturer embarked on a major quality effort in its manufacturing and logistics operations. As part of that program, the company enrolled several hundred employees in a training program covering a broad range of quality techniques. In addition, the manufacturer offered the training to key suppliers and carriers.

All in all, U.S. corporations view personnel investments in a new light today. These firms have reaped the cost reductions and service enhancements available from operational improvements, and are turning to human-resource development as an untapped opportunity for savings. The annual plans of a number of companies now include full-fledged programs to buy or develop specific technical and management skills.

In this vein, a number of companies are discovering that a renewed emphasis on labor-productivity can yield cost savings and service improvements. Elimination of unnecessary or redundant procedures saves time and money. It also improves employee morale and motivation.

Following a major labor-productivity overhaul, one grocery manufacturer's East Coast distribution center now handles more volume in less time, with half the people it had four years ago. It accomplished these improvements without major expenditures for automation.

#5-FORM STRATEGIC ALLIANCES

A fifth principle of logistics excellence calls for companies to form close partnerships with other participants in the product chain. Our research shows that corporations find great value in establishing and sustaining "win-win" linkages with outside parties (brokers, suppliers, distributors, customers) and inside interest (manufacturing, sales, marketing, etc.). This is especially true in Just-in-Time and Quick Response environments in which solid and mutually profitable working relationships are a must.

By way of illustration, one leading consumer-goods manufacturer structures strategic alliances with all primary suppliers as an integral part of its venture-development process. It finds the plusses derived from financial leverage and shared technical expertise improve a venture's profitability. In some cases, these benefits may be the cornerstone of a project's financial viability.

Overall, our research shows that companies are changing the way they view their business alliances. No longer do they consider these relationships short-term, cost-control efforts. Instead, they are cultivating strategic alliances with suppliers, customers, and carriers--even including them in early planning for new ventures.

These partnerships can't succeed without open and timely exchange of information. Companies need to share financial and operational data, as well as forecasting, planning, and scheduling information. In cases we studied, major manufacturers are providing suppliers with "frozen" production schedules a week or two in advance of target shipment dates. Taking advantage of these increased lead times, the suppliers improve service levels. At the same time, the manufacturers reduce raw-material inventory levels.

#6-FOCUS ON FINANCIAL PERFORMANCE

In our two earlier studies, we concluded that the logistics function should use return-on-assets, economic value added, cost and operating standards, or similar financial indicators as measures of performance. This third study confirms this position. Additionally, our research shows that functions such as transportation, warehousing, and customer service are best managed as cost or profit centers. In this way, the company encourages entrepreneurial attitudes among logistics managers.

One of the firms reaping the reward of emphasizing financial performance in logistics is Xerox Corporation. Xerox reduces costs and tailors service levels to the needs of its manufacturing units by creating logistics profit centers that provide the kinds of services its manufacturing executives demand and pay for.

In recent years, U.S. corporations have adopted rate-of-return on assets (ROA) as the most important financial measure of profitability--shifting away from using the net-income yardstick. In line with this shift, some companies are beginning to calculate return on logistics assets, rather than absolute cost levels, as the measure of logistics performance. In addition, these firms find that non-traditional measures such as return on management investment (ROMI) can be useful indicators of logistics performance.

As a direct result of the ROA focus, more companies are using third-party suppliers of logistics service as a means to reduce high logistics-asset investment. According to our research, the motivating factor behind this trend is a reduction in asset levels and improvement in ROA. The recent decline in private truck fleets is directly related to this emphasis on ROA. Similarly, more and more corporations are using public warehousing. A few years ago, those same firms shunned that option.

#7-TARGET OPTIMUM SERVICE LEVELS

Companies that target optimum service levels improve their profitability. Targeting optimum service levels, therefore, should be one of the main elements of a company's logistics strategy. To do this, businesses must quantify the incremental revenue gained from providing excellent customer service, and measure the revenue/cost trade-offs for setting graded service levels. This involves understanding their customers' service needs and expectations and the levels of service they are willing to buy. In other words, companies need to calculate their "optimum" service levels, and pinpoint the costs associated with sustaining those levels. This may lead, for example, to "tiered pricing," wherein different levels of service are priced according to the different costs in reaching them (e.g., delivery times).

Most U.S. firms recognize the competitive importance of customer service. They have established service parameters, and closely monitor how well they meet service commitments. Our research shows that relatively few companies, however, analyze the service requirements of their major markets in sufficient detail to set unique standards appropriate to the competitive requirements of these markets. Such fine-tuning of service parameters helps maximize profitability, as illustrated by the major distributor that increased market share by 2 percent ($440 million in sales) over a three-year period by making selective adjustments to service levels for key product lines in important markets.

As noted above, an increasing number of corporations combine both distribution and materials-management functions under the umbrella of the logistics department. One of the major responsibilities of these combined departments is serving the needs of manufacturing. They manage direct provision of materials, parts, and supplies to manufacturing plants, and handle logistics support for parts and supplies used or sold by field-service organizations.

These integrated operations require the same level of effort in targeting service levels as that expended on external customer service. A case in point is the major distributor who solved an after-the-sale service problem that was eroding market share. The company revamped its service-parts distribution strategy using the same modeling software it used to fine-tune the product distribution network.

In another example, the logistics group of a major electronics manufacturer "contracts" with each of the company's manufacturing divisions for the level of service desired by the division. Through use of a sophisticated transfer-pricing mechanism, the logistics group charges the divisions for whatever levels of service they request.

More and more, the specialized expertise of logistics professionals proves critical in achieving and maintaining smooth operations. The part-time attention given materials management issues when they fall under the control of manufacturing personnel is "too expensive" for many companies.

#8-MANAGE THE DETAILS

Streamlining operations and procedures is important to profitability, but attention to details can mean real savings. The best logistics operations always have the fundamental issues under control, and are constantly resolving seemingly "minor" problems. Collectively, these solutions add up to smooth performance.

Here again, we need to link the details with the business strategy in order to manage the "right details." Corporate logistics policies that dictate the wrong operating practices for customer needs obviously can result in lost sales through seemingly minor inconveniences.

A major supplier to the health care industry has been setting cost/service improvement goals for many years, even though it already enjoys a reputation as a highly cost-effective supplier. When asked when the firm will achieve all the improvements possible, management replied, "We don't know. There seems to be no limit to the creativity of our employees." Management attributes many of the recent improvements to paying attention to details. No aspect of the operations is considered "unimportant."

When it comes to improving operations, simple solutions work best. As one logistics vice president commented when discussing his approach to identifying operational improvements, "If any activity is complicated, there's a better way to do it...and in all likelihood the better way is simpler."

Logistics executives who meet the challenge of integrated logistics realize that complex operations do not have to be complicated--indeed they should not be. At its Buick City automobile plant, General Motors achieved extremely close coordination of its manufacturing operations with the operations of major suppliers and carriers. This interwoven chain of activities would not work had GM not streamlined its entire materials pipeline.

One key to streamlining and simplifying logistics operations is harnessing the knowledge, experience, and creativity of line employees and first-level managers. Our research disclosed that many productivity breakthroughs cited by companies are attributable to involved employees.

In one food-processing firm, a distribution center staffed with self-acknowledged "losers" was transformed into the lowest-cost, highest-quality operation in the company after an enlightened manager successfully convinced workers in the company they could be the "best." Of course, intensive training was an integral part of this success story. The factor that made the difference, however, was the manager's ability to harness the workers' knowledge of the operation and of changes that were possible in the facility.

#9-LEVERAGE LOGISTICS VOLUMES

Our ninth logistics principle specifies that successful logistics operations consolidate shipment volumes, inventories, and the like to gain operating and financial leverage. These consolidations pay off handsomely in terms of improved service and cost performance. To take advantage of these leveraging opportunities, however, management has to analyze every logistics choice and trade-off creatively, looking for new approaches to handling products, markets, modes, carriers, and customers.

Freight consolidation is one of the more popular leveraging methods, our research shows. A new generation of software applications is making dynamic consolidation of shipments an operating reality. Indeed, one computer manufacturer reduced its transportation cost by more than 20 percent using such software, even though it already had a manually operated consolidation program in place.

Reducing the number of carriers used can be an effective way to consolidate volumes. One company pared its outbound carrier pool from several dozen to five, and negotiated strategic alliances with those five carriers on a regional basis. Interestingly, during the whittling-down process, the manufacturer played an instrumental role in mergers among several of the previous carriers. Those mergers proved beneficial to all parties.

As integrated logistics departments evolve, we see increased coordination of inbound- and outbound-shipment volumes. Such coordination usually produces sizeable transportation savings. Once again, real-time information systems make this coordination manageable.

One of the immediate benefits of managing inbound and outbound volumes collectively is improved equipment and driver utilization for private truck fleets. In fact, the significant boost it gives ROA often is the most persuasive argument in favor of implementing such a program.

Excellent logistics operations find that broad-based coordination of all logistics activities, including intra-company transportation, warehousing, and order servicing, can be well worth the trouble. These companies report improvements in customer service and financial performance. One major consumer-goods manufacturer embarked on a multi-year program to distribute several divisions' products through corporate distribution centers. Implementing the program was complicated, but firm management is realizing the kinds of benefits that prove the wisdom of its approach.

#10-MEASURE AND REACT TO PERFORMANCE

Once achieved, logistics excellence must be sustained or gains will be short-lived. Companies must measure their logistics performance and react to the measurement results in an ongoing, dynamic fashion.

The most effective logistics operations are those linking their operating procedures directly to their overall logistics strategy. That logistics strategy is, in turn, linked to the corporate strategy. The corporate strategic goals form the basis for management identification of the levels of performance necessary for success, and how best to measure that performance.

This approach guarantees that logistics activities mesh with marketing and manufacturing initiatives. More than one company has learned the value of coordinating logistics, marketing, and manufacturing strategies the hard way. These companies reduced the number of warehouses to cut inventories and improve ROA, only to discover the resulting market-share losses wiped out any cost savings.

Without constant attention and fine-tuning, performance measurements soon decay into oblivion. Although every company is quick to acknowledge that logistics is a very dynamic function, few reflect this dynamic environment in their monitoring of the adequacy of their performance measures. Our research shows that the excellent logistics managers don't just review performance; they require people to explain variances and analyze the appropriateness of the performance standard.

THE RESULT

As we suggested earlier, we like to refer to these principles of logistics excellence as "uncommon sense." Indeed, most executives take these principles for granted, to the point where they neglect to include them in their standard operating procedures.

We are convinced that applying these principles and thereby achieving excellence in logistics can and does improve corporate profitability. Where logistics operations follow the principles by conducting activities linked to business objectives, we see quantitative improvements in measures such as:

- Compound asset growth
- Compound equity growth
- Market to book (wealth creation)
- Return to total capital
- Return on equity
- Return on sales
- Return on management investment
- Economic value added
- Market share

In the next 10 chapters, we discuss how these measures are directly affected by innovative applications of our 10 principles of logistics excellence. We describe each of the 10 maxims in more detail, and provide case examples of how logistics innovations have impacted corporate profitability directly.

PART II: PRINCIPLES OF LOGISTICS EXCELLENCE

Chapter 3
LINKING LOGISTICS TO CORPORATE STRATEGY

As summarized in Chapter 2, the first and foremost guideline for achieving logistics profit-improvement potential is the integration of logistics operations with the business strategy on an ongoing basis. One business-unit president told us that this principle was so obvious it did not bear discussion. Yet when we studied his company, we discovered that although appearing adequate at first glance, the linkages between corporate strategy and logistics were barely adequate and less than successful.

The president's company was a medium-sized firm producing lighting products for institutional and residential use. Its new corporate business strategy focused on promoting growth in target market segments. Management executed that strategy through focused marketing, selective pricing and promotion, and a manufacturing efficiency-improvement program. Because the corporate parent had set up ambitious financial goals for the business unit, top management was directly involved in executing the strategy.

When we assessed the logistics operations, however, we discovered certain weaknesses in the strategy linkages. First we found the company relied on indirect distribution channels for getting its products to market. Specifically, it sold through dealers and distributors, who were not adequately briefed on the company's targeted marketing, pricing, and promotion programs. These outlets sold to any available customer in their territories, rather than focusing their efforts around the new programs. This caused confusion among customers and diluted the impact of the company's new initiatives. We also discovered that management paid minimal attention to distribution efficiency. The company invested heavily in production improvement, implementing extensive Manufacturing Resource Planning (MRP) systems with some success. MRP, however, did not help the firm plan what and where to produce (the company had multi-plant locations), what finished goods to stock and where, and from which warehouse to ship. No Distribution Resource Planning (DRP) systems were in place, so management was uncertain as to how much inventory to stock, and where. As a result, transportation and inventory-carrying costs were excessively high relative to the company's sales, products, and distribution channels.

The firm's sales and marketing, distribution, and production departments were not well coordinated. The disorganization created by this environment generated problems in fulfilling the corporate strategy. For instance, customers perceived the unit's performance as inconsistent, a perception that eroded their confidence in the company's ability to process orders.

The firm's various departments operated on different information. Consequently, flexibility needed to meet changing customer needs was virtually nonexistent. And, distribution performance, i.e., how well products were being delivered to customers (including dealers), was measured on the basis of physical factors, such as units handled per labor hour, which were unrelated to customers' actual needs. These and other logistics deficiencies produced higher-than-necessary operating costs, and lower-than-projected sales.

When we reported the above operational realities to the firm's president, he revised his opinion of logistics, and instituted changes that improved the linkage between logistics and corporate strategy. After operating under these changes for six months, costs were down, service levels improved, and sales in targeted marketing segments increased.

For one reason or another, this lack of strategy linkage appears all too frequently in American industry today. Even where logistics appears well managed, we find that a proper challenge of how well the function is linked to the business strategy yields opportunities for profit improvement. As a result, it is always worthwhile to explore how the principle of linkage works, and how companies can benefit from it.

THE STATE OF CORPORATE STRATEGY

Nearly every business periodical published today discusses at length the ills plaguing American manufacturing, and offers a selection of remedies. What companies need, they say, is "excellence," "quality," "one-minute managers," "Japanese management styles," or any number of popular techniques for saving U.S. industry.

One of the most concise descriptions of American industry's problems was prepared by the National Research Council's Manufacturing Studies Board, headed by a retired top executive of General Electric, with members from companies such as Deere & Co. and Procter & Gamble. The Board stated that:

> *"...U.S. manufacturing is in danger of being unprepared to compete in the coming age, a failure that would result in rapid erosion of the U.S. manufacturing base....Manufacturing companies will have to become far more flexible, efficient, and responsive to market conditions....The time lag between design and production, and from order to delivery, must shrink dramatically. Dynamic, continuous improvements in capabilities will become essential to long-term success...."* [4]

The report from the Board also stressed that "technology is not a miracle worker," and that companies must break down barriers such as organizational and management sterility and myopia, and replace them with dynamic, integrated systems. Strict job classifications must be eliminated and communication links among internal divisions, suppliers, and customers improved. "Every company will have access to advanced technology," the Board observed. "The competitive difference will be based on how well it is used."

Corporate business strategy must respond to this theme over the next decade. During the 1960s and '70s, strategy focused on specialization, centralization, and internal growth. It often addressed goals other than customer service. Customer service suffered as a result, and dissatisfied clients turned to other producers.

In light of these less-than-successful past strategic focuses, it is instructive to look at what criteria today's venture capitalists use to evaluate investment alternatives. A recent New York University survey found that venture capitalists look for the following characteristics in a firm.[5] In order of importance, they specify that the best firms for investment:

1. Are capable of sustained effort

2. Are thoroughly familiar with the market

3. Offer at least 10 times return on investment in 5-10 years

4. Have demonstrated leadership in the past

5. Evaluate and react well to risk

6. Permit investment to be made liquid

7. Record significant market growth

8. Show a good track record relevant to investment

9. Articulate the investment well

10. Offer proprietary protection

Shareholders express similar requirements of a firm, i.e., efficient management, healthy profits, fair dividends, and good communications. These criteria characterize a company type that is far different from what was created in the '60s and early '70s. Corporate strategies then promoted large bureaucracies, ignored innovative business opportunities, and fostered underutilization of company assets.

The pressing need to remedy the shortcomings produced by poor product/service quality and inadequately sustained effort in the marketplace are creating a new environment for corporate strategy. This environment, we believe, is characterized by the following strategic goals, all of which require significant change in American industry's standard operating procedure. Companies will have to:

- **Establish better-perceived product and service quality.** In order to maximize profit and growth advantage, a company's product/service must not only be "good," it must be perceived to be better than those of its competitors. This will be the key to sustainable top performance.

- **Create a global orientation toward business growth and performance.** In the future, experts predict that 70 percent of the solutions to today's business problems will come from outside the United States. Labor, material, and component problems, which occupy significant executive time today, will be resolved with foreign sourcing. Reaction time to worldwide business events will shrink as a result.

- **Streamline and integrate company operations to become more flexible, efficient, and productive.** Regardless of the strategy adopted for competitive advantage--cost leadership, premium service, or both--there will be a clear progression toward improved ability to react to customers' needs in an efficient and effective manner. Achieving this integration will require reorganization, judicious use of technology, and a new management style. It will be a key factor for survival.

These three strategic goals--quality, global orientation, and integration--do not necessarily comprise the sum of corporate strategy for the next decade. Each company will have its own, more specific strategy agenda. These specific agendas, however, will take a back seat to the three larger issues cited above. We see this trend emerging already at companies such as General Motors, Ford, and Chrysler.

Corporate strategy, then, will be directed increasingly toward managing change for the purpose of gaining and sustaining competitive advantage. One of its key focuses will be understanding and meeting the real needs of customers. We must avoid the traps of merely targeting **perceived** needs or replicating the service levels of the industry leader. We believe this emphasis favors, among other things, the effective use of logistics to achieve the level of customer-service quality that yields higher sales and profits.

THE STATE OF LOGISTICS STRATEGY

As is the case with overall corporate strategy, logistics strategy since the early 1970s has addressed goals and objectives that frequently are counterproductive in today's markets. Often companies pursue productivity gains and cost reductions to the detriment of customer service or market flexibility. Basically, this situation stems from the perception of logistics as a cost center in which cost control is paramount as long as a minimum service level is maintained.

Prior to deregulation of the transportation industry in 1980, physical distribution in most companies was limited to getting finished products to customers by whatever means available. This usually meant using the surface mode--motor or railroad--that had the operating authority to handle the shipment and was the favored supplier. Cost and service negotiation was not an issue because tariffs were regulated.

The logistics-strategy environment during the early '80s followed a similar track. It was driven by cost consciousness, especially regarding the number and location of facilities (i.e., warehouses, distribution centers, or stocking locations). Most companies constructed a distribution network that placed a premium on minimizing the costs of getting products to customers.

Logistics managers, with the help of computer models, have become adept at analyzing cost trade-offs involved in warehousing versus transportation. Because of the physical nature of logistics, i.e., the storing, handling, and moving of materials and products, evaluation of logistics-strategy alternatives lends itself to computer-based decision support. The development of such computer models has progressed to the point where the best ones can simulate hundreds of stockkeeping units (SKUs) being delivered to thousands of customers from multi-echelon distribution networks (plants, distribution centers, field warehouses, etc.).

These computer tools have evolved to the point where they now can analyze multiple logistics-strategy alternatives on a regular basis. The reason more companies do not take advantage of this technology is hard to pinpoint. The answer may lie in the fact that most logistics executives have not convinced top management that carefully meshing logistics-strategy alternatives with marketing, sales, and manufacturing strategies can contribute to profitability.

Use of creative logistics alternatives will help companies respond to the four major strategic issues they face. These innovations can help firms:

- **Establish better-recognized quality of customer service.** To sustain top performance, the logistics function must support the company by providing a level of service to customers that will differentiate the company from its competitors. On-time deliveries and complete orders are only part of this service commitment. Logistics managers must determine and deliver what the customer needs and is willing to pay for in the way of service.

- **Continually evaluate international logistics in terms of current operations and future opportunities.** Successful companies use materials, components, and labor with high performance/cost relationships. They target attractive markets worldwide for their products. These policies affect logistics costs and services dramatically, increasing the need for logistics evaluations.

- **Bring to the logistics function a high degree of flexibility, efficiency, and productivity.** In order to operate in these spheres, logistics managers must work harder and smarter. Old methods are becoming obsolete, and having the lowest-cost distribution network will not be enough to secure competitive advantage. Logistics strategies will have to create the right levels of service, for the right customers, at the right time, and at acceptable cost.

- **Understand the total economics of getting or not getting a sale.** Often the pursuit or acceptance of additional business is based on the gross margins involved. Better understanding of the true "below-the-line" distribution costs involved leads to more profitable decisions.

GUIDELINES FOR AND BENEFITS OF LINKING STRATEGIES AND LOGISTICS OPERATIONS

The logistics strategy should parallel corporate strategy, reflecting the broad issues and objectives important to the business. More importantly, however, the logistics functions should be linked directly and specifically to the corporate strategy, as our principle of logistics excellence states.

Framework for Strategy-Focused Operations

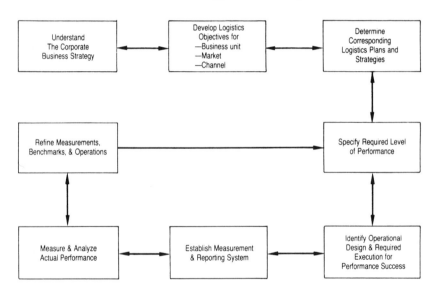

Ideally, the successful linking of logistics with the corporate business strategy follows a process like the one illustrated above, labeled the "framework for strategy-focused operations." Each "box" in the process represents a linkage step--forward and backward--that allows logistics operations to be driven by, and contribute to, the corporate business strategy. We developed this framework as a result of our work with several leading logistics departments. Let's consider each step in the framework in terms of what it might involve and how these leading companies implement it.

Understand the Corporate Business Strategy. Not all manufacturing, merchandising, or distribution companies have a formal, current, and comprehensive strategic plan. Most companies, however, have at least set some type of long-term business direction and logistics managers must understand it if they are to support it effectively.

A common element in most corporate strategies is competitive advantage--either how to gain it or how to protect it. Often, aggressive strategic steps targeting manufacturing, marketing, and financial actions necessary to outstrip the competition are laid out. In leading companies the head of logistics is an integral part of this process.

In many consumer-products companies, value-added activities in materials management, distribution, and customer service are key elements of the corporation's strategic plan. New quality and service goals are highlighting the visibility and importance of logistics, since it plays a major role in their achievement.

The key to accomplishing strategy-focused logistics operations is identifying and understanding the major elements of the company's strategy. Leading logistics executives pay particular attention to the following areas:

- **Market share.** What quantitative goals are being set and how do they vary by geographic area, customer type, and distribution channel?

- **Financial results.** What goals are being established for overall profit, cost levels, and return on assets or investment?

- **New products/markets.** How important are new products and markets, and how readily can existing logistics networks and practices support their introduction?

- **New technology.** Are new technologies that are key to achieving corporate strategic goals compatible with existing logistics strategies and operations and has logistics been adequately considered in developing these technologies?

- **Growth/divestment.** What strategies are being considered that could require major restructuring of existing logistics networks? Are there options being considered that present significant logistics opportunities or problems?

We identified one industrial-goods manufacturer, for example, who advocates an informal strategy of "hold our own," i.e., the firm tries to hold steady its position on market share, sales, revenue, profits, or returns. In today's highly competitive environment, this might indeed be an effective goal; but it is **not** a strategy until the ways in which the company expects to hold its own are spelled out in detailed financial and operational terms. Making the general commitment to "continue doing what got us here," as this company did, is frequently not enough. Markets, customers, and competition continue to change, in ways that compel innovative responses from us.

Logistics managers must understand the corporate priorities, and work to influence top management in identifying the strategic steps needed to achieve those goals. Along with sales and marketing, logistics people are closest to customers. They are well positioned to understand the marketplace. For that reason, they must play a role in determining the firm's strategic direction.

Develop Operating Objectives for the Logistics Function. Understanding and influencing the business strategy is of primary importance to the overall company, but that by itself is inadequate. Each major functional group--marketing, sales, operations, logistics, and finance--must develop integrated and realistic operating objectives that spell out how the corporate strategy will be achieved. For example, competitive differentiation can result, in part, from service or cost leadership. Some companies have set their sights on being the absolute low-cost supplier. Others strive to be the premier service supplier, e.g., Frito-Lay. Targeting both objectives simultaneously makes no sense. To be effective, strategic objectives must ultimately guide operational decisions.

When, at three in the afternoon, a warehouse manager is faced with unfilled orders that are scheduled for shipment today, what response is best? An absolute low-cost supplier strategy suggests ship tomorrow. A premier service supplier would work overtime. It is through this basic operationalization of strategic objectives that logistics excellence is achieved **and** sustained.

Integrating strategic objectives among functional groups provides a synergy that is often critical to achieving corporate strategic goals. Current fascination with the "Just-in-Time" (JIT) manufacturing/distribution concept illustrates this point. Many U.S. manufacturing processes are dramatically inefficient when compared to those of Japanese firms. About 95 percent of in-process work in American factories is lost in idle time, i.e., parts moving from one operation to another, or waiting for the next machining operation. Leading American corporations, such as General Motors, Whirlpool, Hewlett-Packard, IBM, and Black & Decker, have made tangible advances in improving the manufacturing process through implementation of techniques to reduce inventory, lead times, and set-up times, along with ways to re-arrange machines by product and function, to increase labor productivity, and to achieve total quality control.

Adoption of a JIT philosophy or strategy requires long-term top-management support and total employee involvement. Commitment must be total because adoption of JIT methods requires changes in philosophy, attitudes, and work habits, company-wide. Most **Fortune** 1000 companies are reviewing or experimenting with JIT. Indeed, many feel that adopting its basic tenets is key to remaining viable in the face of worldwide competition.

In looking at JIT operations, we often find they do not encompass the logistics flows, both inbound and outbound. Management pays so much attention to the shop floor (admittedly for good reason) that it overlooks opportunities in supply and delivery, although that is the very area where logistics managers should be influencing **and** implementing JIT strategy.

Significant results can accrue if JIT is applied to logistics. Leaseway Transportation Corp., for example, provides Whirlpool with JIT movement of raw materials, goods-in-process, and finished products to and among its plants and distribution centers. Frequent small deliveries of parts and materials on an on-time basis, and a service-intensive relationship, save Whirlpool substantial monies on capital investment and inventory carrying costs.

The Whirlpool-Leaseway arrangement also provides for a lean, streamlined manufacturing and distribution flow. Specifically, Whirlpool logistics managers specify operating objectives reflecting the company's overall JIT business strategy. Leaseway helps management achieve these goals. As a result, Whirlpool achieves (and sustains) a cost **and** service advantage through logistics operations that are integrated with the company's business and manufacturing strategy.

Determine Corresponding Operations Plans and Strategies. Setting operating objectives for logistics is the step that links logistics strategy with the corporate business strategy. In the 1980s, it has become more commonplace for functional areas of a company to develop operating plans and strategies for their respective units. Consequently, logistics/distribution plans have sprung up in company after company. More often than not, however, these plans and strategies are not properly integrated with the other business functions of production, sales and marketing, and information management.

Why is this the case? Logistics managers should be the first to realize the necessity of coordinating activities and information with other departments precisely because they deal with the physical flow of materials and products through the business. We often found they did realize the need for coordination, but fell prey to organizational, technical, financial, or timing constraints which prevented proper integration.

In such cases, corporate profitability is at stake. Logistics by its very nature involves complex interactions among purchasing, production scheduling, warehousing, transportation, and inventory. Achieving real integration of logistics with other functions--marketing, sales, and production--is a challenge, to be sure. But we have seen (and helped) numerous companies do just that. These successes prove the benefits of the endeavor.

A major foods-processor client provides a case in point. What began as an assessment of its logistics systems (in the beginning, finished-goods distribution only) evolved into a comprehensive logistics strategy for the entire business unit (over $2 billion in sales).

By elevating management interest in the corporate benefits of logistics excellence, we helped redefine the scope of logistics to its broadest definition (i.e., inbound and outbound flows), encouraged management to include production operations in the project, and encouraged the firm to view operations management with an eye toward integration. The company is enthusiastically pursuing this strategy because its detailed financial projections of its costs and benefits showed major advances, including:

- Reductions in costs and asset investment

- Fostering introduction of new products

- More flexibility in responding to targeted marketing and promotional initiatives

- Improved customer service and sales increases

Adopting this approach, and the improvements in systems that go with it, are putting the company in the enviable position of managing the product "from the grain field to the pantry." This control will give the firm a competitive advantage in cost, service, and quality.

Specify Required Level of Performance. In visiting with companies, we noticed that many do a respectable job developing logistics objectives that parallel and reflect the corporate business strategy. They also create a logistics plan to meet these objectives. At that point, unfortunately, they stop. Apparently, management believes the plan will manage itself, so managers sit back until the next year or next planning period, when they repeat the goal-setting process.

Avoiding a blizzard of monthly budget and performance reports is a goal common among logistics managers. They want to manage operations, not paperwork. No matter how good a plan is, however, it can't manage itself. The key to concise performance monitoring is specifying the exact levels of performance required to meet our strategic objectives. Leading-edge logistics organizations, like those at Xerox, Johnson & Johnson, and Nabisco-Brands, set and monitor "key indicators" as a regular component of their logistics planning and control process. To do so involves specifying ahead of time the detailed performance objectives established for the following areas:

- **Volumes.** What percentage of outbound volume will be shipped by each mode? What levels of key materials and supplies inventories will be maintained in each storeroom? What level of peak-period, overflow warehouse capacity is necessary to minimize the company's warehouse investment?

- **Service levels.** What customer-service measures should be used at each order-servicing point? What values (e.g., fill rates or cycle times) should be targeted? What level of parts or raw materials availability is needed to support manufacturing or field-service operations?

- **Cost/financial investment.** What cost levels are acceptable for transportation, warehousing, inventory carrying, and administration? What investment in logistics assets is necessary to meet ROA goals? What asset and labor productivity levels are needed to achieve established cost and financial targets?

Such performance indicators or measures are designed for two purposes:

1) To provide performance criteria in designing or refining logistics facilities and operating procedures.

2) To provide early warning when we are in danger of missing logistics objectives for the period.

Identify Operational Design and Required Execution for Performance Success. As we said, companies often fail to take performance goals to the next level--that of determining the mix of resources, processes, technology, and other factors needed to meet the goals. This level of detail identifies exactly how logistics will function during the planning period, and includes an estimate of resources needed to execute the program.

It is at this point, with performance goals clearly in mind, that logistics leaders fine-tune their operations. They challenge their past practices and make needed modifications to bring them in line with strategic goals. This presents a major opportunity to streamline operations and reduce cost.

Many U.S. companies have grown inefficient and have become burdened with high overhead, such that their overall cost performance is uncompetitive. In such cases, cost cutting is necessary, but it must be accomplished without killing the business. We found that when faced with this situation, leading companies threw away old practices and emphasized innovation and linkages with strategic plans. They challenged reporting relationships and assignments of responsibility. Nothing was sacred! Practices like "we've always done it this way" were particular targets. Their goals went beyond mere cost reduction. They restructured "mission-critical" practices and systems to eliminate elements that were not supporting strategic objectives.

Logistics operations, representing up to 50 percent of total costs, provide important opportunities to achieve cost containment while meeting required service levels. In Chapter 9, we discuss in more detail how the best logistics organizations target "optimum service levels." The challenge lies in specifying the right amount of resources and technology (costs) needed to achieve performance goals. Tailoring operations to strategy is critical.

A leading consumer-products company that has adopted quality consultant Philip Crosby's "cost of quality" model is a useful example of this specification process. Although this company already has a well-deserved reputation for top-quality products, management found it valuable to expand the definition of "quality" to its logistics operations. When they did, they were shocked at what doing things wrong can cost in terms of product returns, time spent placating customers, late deliveries, incomplete orders, and the like. If more logistics managers followed this approach, and showed their people why tasks should be done right the first time, logistics costs would shrink.

Take care, however. An excessive application of cost containment when aligning operations with strategy can create problems. We saw cases where a company's purchasing department only bought from the supplier with the lowest product price. In the long run, this policy proved expensive when related logistics and quality costs were not considered. For example, one company decreased its inspection and reworking costs by weeding out vendors who failed to supply top-quality components consistently. The remaining core group of high-quality suppliers were rewarded for their efforts with larger orders. Larger order quantities, in turn, gave the purchasing department more price leverage and increased shipment sizes, thereby gaining additional transportation cost savings.

A more subtle example of overzealous low-price fixation occurs when purchasing decisions are made based on costs only, without considering vendor proximity to the plant. One well-known food company cancelled a supplier on a price decision even though the vendor was located directly across the street from a plant, and the replacement supplier was hundreds of miles away. We evaluated this buying decision in light of the cost of delayed production runs caused by late or incomplete shipments. This loss of flexibility and the resulting inventory build-up and adverse sales impacts showed materials management the real cost of its short-sighted buying policy. Management became a strong advocate of linking operational decisions to its underlying strategic objectives.

Establish Measurement and Reporting Systems. Often, logistics and other managers downplay the performance measurement and reporting steps involved in implementing a strategic plan. They do so not because these steps are unimportant, but because they are comfortable with and accustomed to using traditional reports and measures. This frequently occurs when companies acquire packaged software (distribution requirements planning or transportation management, for example) and accept the "packaged" performance measures and reports as gospel.

This feeling of comfort, however, is not universal. Ernst & Whinney has been conducting a number of client seminars on the subject of logistics performance. During the seminars, logistics, sales, production, and financial managers frequently get into heated exchanges on what really is important to their business. These discussions invariably highlight the tendency to evaluate the "adequacy" of operations from our own functional perspective. They also surface the frustrations that unfailingly result when we do so.

A major electronics manufacturer has successfully addressed this problem by making normal operational trade-offs a part of its planning process and setting performance goals for each function reflecting those planned trade-offs. Thus when they agreed to spend more on transportation to support a shift to regional rather than national promotions, the transportation budget reflected that planned increase.

In another case, a consumer-products firm was planning to introduce new software systems. During discussions on the business needs surrounding these systems, conversation touched on all the issues of responsibility, authority, measurement goals, accountability, information overload, old versus new ways of doing business, and timing of measurements. As a result, the firm instituted cross-organizational working sessions in order to resolve problematic issues prior to introducing the new software. These sessions identified modifications to the packaged software, and set up a program whereby modifications will be designed "up front" to mirror company operations and required levels of performance.

In every company, measurement and reporting systems must be continually challenged to ensure they stay aligned with strategic objectives. At one of the largest U.S. corporations, logistics managers are starting to question whether the traditional measures of distribution performance are adequate for today's needs. During the past decade, distribution analysts developed a set of standard measures to gauge operating performance, including:

- Cases (units) handled
- Inventory (product, SKU) turns
- Labor productivity (warehouse)
- Shipping and receiving productivity
- Costs by warehouse activity, i.e., receiving, checking, put-away, etc.

Although these measures tell us "how we're doing" internally, they fail to assess how well we are serving customers.

If we want to emphasize customer service, getting close to our customers, and other customer-oriented efforts, shouldn't we measure how well we serve our customers? To do this, we must institute measures of on-time deliveries, order-fill rates, and service during promotions. (See Chapter 9 for a more detailed discussion of this.)

Measure and Analyze Performance. Obviously, it does little good to establish measurement systems if we don't read the reports, assess what they mean, and determine the reasons for variances from expected results. We certainly want to know "how we did." More importantly, however, we want to know "why we didn't do as well as we expected."

As mentioned, we at Ernst & Whinney see too many companies doing a good job of planning and monitoring their logistics operations, but failing to follow up adequately on performance problems. Why does this happen? Usually, logistics managers are uncertain why a variance occurred, are misled by inaccurate reports, or focus on the "wrong" problems. It does little good for profitability to change warehouse stocking locations--a move that might be indicated based on reports of slow picking locations--if a more critical problem such as an excessive number of incomplete or inaccurate orders being shipped to customers is not detected before sales erode. Many existing reporting procedures do not identify the significant variances, much less the right issues or opportunities.

Xerox, Johnson & Johnson, and other industry leaders have structured their performance reporting systems to highlight **significant** variances while avoiding proliferation of reports and meaningless detail. Many of these organizations readily admit that their systems were not always that focused. Universally they have found, however, that when the emphasis is put on taking corrective action rather than just reporting results, measurement systems became leaner **and** more effective.

Refine Measurements, Benchmarks, and Operations. The last "box" on our strategy-focused operations diagram emphasizes the need to use reports to bring results in line with performance objectives. This requires adjusting or "fine-tuning" logistics operations to achieve expected results. As the **action** step in the process, this is the point at which management takes the necessary action to correct, refine, or change some procedures in a logistics activity to improve the operation.

Unfortunately, our research shows that most logistics managers shy away from the operational-process details, and attempt to correct per-

40

formance problems through either better planning or "one-minute manager" coaching. Neither solution gets to the heart of the process problem. What is needed is a change in measurements, procedures, or both. (See Chapter 10 for more on managing the details.)

As an example, one consumer-goods manufacturer had set a marketing strategy that shifted emphasis from "order taking" to merchandising support as one of its key elements. Management trained its sales force to work with retail buyers on promotional and advertising programs. Initial customer response was very favorable, but subsequent problems arose which turned the entire program into a marketing disaster. Stores were increasingly out of stock on heavily promoted items, creating frustration among store managers and consumers who were responding to the ads and promotions. What was the source of the problem? Its key cause was a failure to align distribution performance measures and operations with the new marketing strategy. Field managers were still targeting old cost and service goals that had not been updated.

This was not a simple communications problem. The new marketing strategy was well known to many distribution managers. The problem arose because certain linkages necessary to achieve true strategy-focused operations had been overlooked.

THE RIGHT PERSPECTIVE

We suggested earlier that the linkage principle--our first and most important guideline for achieving logistics' profit-improvement potential--is the best example of how the 10 principles of logistics excellence represent "uncommon sense." It may seem surprising that so few companies have succeeded in linking logistics directly to the corporate strategy. Nevertheless, the fact remains that logistics, like manufacturing, has lagged behind the more glamorous company functions of marketing, finance, and mergers and acquisitions in providing strategic or competitive advantage.

What factor has the greatest influence on a company's ability to retain its customer franchise? Is the company's strategic objective to remain or become the low-cost producer? To meet customers' needs for consistent service quality? To be the new-products innovator? The operational answers to these questions have been neglected for too long. However, they provide the basis for differentiating the company from its competitors. More than ever, top management understands that this differentiation is critical to a firm's survival.

Chapter 4
ORGANIZING COMPREHENSIVELY

Perhaps no subject in internal corporate life generates as much attention and concern as the design and structure of the organization chart. Scholars and organizational consultants have written endless treatises on the theory of organization, its effects on corporate culture, and on the pros and cons of one structure or another. As major corporate functions, logistics, materials management, and physical distribution frequently are the subject of such debates.

The logistics function, however, may illustrate better than any other corporate activity the intensity with which the organizational issues at a company are addressed. Why is this? Because logistics--with its broad-based responsibilities associated with the flow of raw materials through the organization to the customer--touches (and often conflicts with) many other corporate activities. The figure below illustrates typical conflicts that may arise.

As the logistics function continues to undergo a "quiet revolution," its organization structure becomes more challenging. Even as we conducted the research for this book, we observed leading companies like Xerox, Johnson & Johnson, IBM, and General Motors changing their logistics organizations.

These corporate giants are not the only firms making changes. Hundreds of other companies have revised their logistics organizations in response to transportation deregulation, increased management awareness of logistics opportunities, or organizational realignments. As one logistics executive said to us, "Reorganization? The real question is what organizational change have we made this month!"

To eliminate the kinds of "conflicts of interest" that arise from logistics' broad sphere of influence, most innovative companies address the logistics organization in an integrated context. They recognize the essential interrelationships between logistics, manufacturing, marketing, sales, and finance. In this process they seek to foster **joint** goal setting to emphasize synergistic opportunities rather than simply to minimize conflicts of interest. This means the firm identifies what functions or activities comprise logistics and pinpoints how they are best integrated and managed to support and enhance the combined efforts of all company activities.

Functional Interests & Impacts: Conflict Management

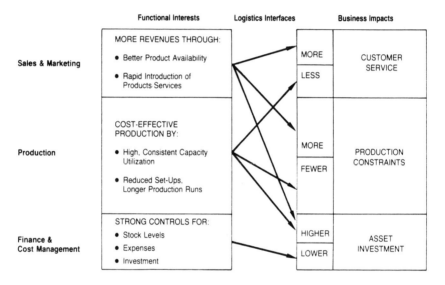

The value-chain concept, which creates a pipeline by linking value-added activities, provides a useful framework for conducting such an organizational analysis. It, along with other assessment criteria, such as asset utilization and productivity goals, can help management create the company organization structure that is most responsive to internal and external customers. Let's consider these principles and factors with regard to the comprehensive logistics organization, and look at how such a structure can improve profitability.

EVOLUTION OF THE BUSINESS LOGISTICS ORGANIZATION

Despite increasing corporate understanding that close coordination among operating units is necessary in order to minimize conflicts and make accurate cost trade-offs (e.g., transportation versus inventory), relatively few companies today consolidate logistics activities under a single organizational umbrella. This lack of consolidation is due largely to the fact that many companies are still split operationally and emotionally into two camps--manufacturing and sales/marketing. They do not really appreciate the profit advantages of achieving a smooth, continuous flow from materials sources through operations to customers. Thus they align the materials management organization with manufacturing and physical distribution with sales and marketing.

As recently as the early 1980s, only a handful of leading companies thought of logistics in terms of a pipeline similar to that shown below. (We attribute this pipeline concept to Professor Bernard La Londe of Ohio State University, who advanced the theory some ten years ago.[6])

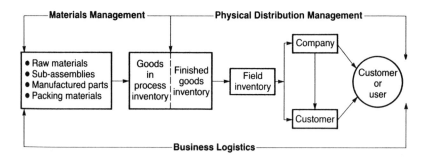

Throughout the 1970s, as companies began to better understand the interrelationship of the materials, inventory, and product flows, several companies improved their competitive position by addressing the pipeline from a planning standpoint. These firms calculated and measured costs, and identified the proper number and locations of facilities. Functional integration, however, stopped there. They made very few organizational changes to reflect the complete pipeline flow itself.

What did evolve from the 1970s was a centralization of distribution management, and the creation of positions such as vice president of distribution. In a few innovative companies, the distribution executive was "equal" in stature to the vice presidents of marketing, manufacturing, engineering, finance, and the like. Typically, this distribution organization looked something like the one illustrated below, although only the more aggressive distribution departments included information systems specialists, financial/controller personnel, and dedicated planning staff to handle the unique needs of finished-goods distribution. Most distribution organizations relied on support for these areas from people assigned elsewhere who had only a "dotted-line" relationship with distribution.

A Typical Organization: Distribution Function

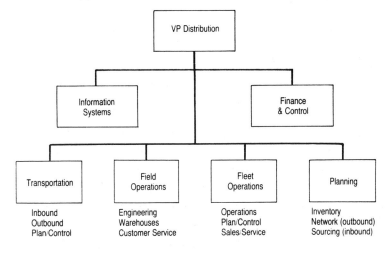

Although this organization structure is relatively comprehensive in that it includes finished-goods planning and operations, it falls short of the logistics-organization ideal. That ideal calls for the control of all logistics functions under a single business unit, using an appropriate mix of centralized and decentralized decision making, with appropriate personnel and systems to support the decision-making process. A possible "ideal" organization is illustrated below.

An Ideal Logistics Organization

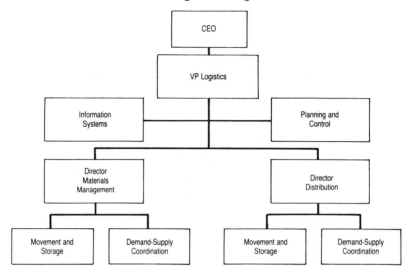

Of course, each company's organizational strategy must reflect the special characteristics inherent to the firm, such as its corporate culture and performance measurement system. In fact, a structure that works at one company may not succeed at another, even if the two firms are similar in size and product type. Take, for example, the case of one large grocery manufacturer who tried to regain lost market share, in part, by emulating the highly centralized distribution organization of a leading competitor. The strategy was partially successful. The distribution network was rationalized and finished-goods inventory levels dropped under centralized control. Problems emerged, however, in transportation because the headquarters transportation staff were too far removed from their decentralized manufacturing and field distribution operations to fully provide needed support and cost control. The competitor's more centralized management of manufacturing and smaller number of plants accommodated a more centralized approach to distribution.

THE LOGISTICS CULTURE

Many executives we interviewed stressed how important corporate culture and values are to an organization's health. Our interviews with leading executives showed that, regardless of the effectiveness of the logistics functions or the people who manage them, the social dimensions of the organization dictate its health. They encompass several elements:

- Senior management's vision of the company's future.

- Corporate philosophy on responsibilities to customers, employees, investors, suppliers, and local communities.

- Prevailing management styles that are fostered and encouraged.

- Values that have been instilled and are shared throughout the organization.

Their chief role is establishing common corporate objectives and fundamental means of achieving them. These are critical to achieving the synergism among internal departments and strategic partners that yields and sustains long-term profitability and business success.

Further, these objectives must be freely communicated by management (throughout the organization) in practice and example as well as in concept. Top management's style and leadership, in particular, determine how important organizational structure is to the company.

Top management style must foster an awareness, particularly among middle managers, of the need to coordinate activities with other departments on a day-to-day basis. At one high-tech electronics company, we observed a marked lack of coordination among purchasing, transportation, and production--to the point that information was protected, not shared. The firm's logistics culture was isolationist. Managers perceived their interests as best served by setting unit-level performance goals. For example, they established a top priority of being the lowest-cost operator, regardless of how that priority affected other departments. No single executive or management team at the company reviewed performance in terms of broader, cross-unit results. Consequently, the business had internal problems that even its customers noticed.

When we consult with logistics executives, we always suggest they "clean up their own house" before attempting to reorganize. This involves clearly defining the logistics goals, objectives, and plans they have adopted to support those same elements at the corporate level. Often a simple, pragmatic approach is the best way of accomplishing this. Burroughs Corporation did just that several years ago.[7] The computer systems manufacturer wanted to "get close to its customers." In reviewing how it might achieve this objective, logistics management noticed that few people involved in order filling, warehousing, transportation, and the like knew what produced customer satisfaction. Nor did they know how their activities impacted customer relations.

To solve this basic, yet critical, problem, management implemented a poster campaign aimed at educating logistics employees as to what makes customers happy. The posters focused on key logistics factors such as accuracy, precision, courtesy, excellence, appearance, teamwork, and communications. Two such posters contained the following messages:

ACCURACY

- Accuracy is paperwork that's filled out correctly and completely.
- Accuracy is being sure of the facts when you are in contact with a customer.
- Accuracy sustains our company's good reputation!

EXCELLENCE

- Excellence is products and service that reflect the highest standards.

- Excellence is teamwork, appearance, communication, accuracy, dependability, courtesy, and precision.

- Excellence is where our company's reputation begins!

Burroughs's "poster of the month" program, together with related coaching sessions among logistics teams and achievement rewards, dramatically changed the logistics organization's culture. As the vice president of logistics told us, "Awareness leads to concern; concern leads to action; action leads to results; and results are measurable." Simple, but effective.

ORGANIZATION FOLLOWS STRATEGY

One of the basic principles of management--usually recognized but rarely adhered to--holds that a company's organizational structure should be linked directly to its business strategy. As we pointed out in the previous chapter, a strategy-focused logistics operation is the key to excellence and profitability. Logically, then, the logistics organization must be organized to carry out this mission.

Companies can no longer afford to view organization structure as a rigid definition of hierarchical levels. Instead, departments should be organized in the way that best communicates and implements the strategic direction. This means management must design the logistics organization around the company's situation, i.e., the competitors it faces, the tasks it needs to undertake, and the people required to perform the tasks.

Although some firms view this concept as too theoretical, the underlying thought process involved is logical and pragmatic. It continually challenges whether the organizational groupings of existing managers and staff and the assignments of responsibilities among these groups are the most effective for performing the plans and activities we have chosen as being the best ways to meet our goals and objectives. For example, we may target superior customer service and resulting sales improvement as important to meeting profit goals. If so, service impacts become key criteria in making organizational decisions.

We can point to several examples where this basic thought process has worked well in targeting organizational decisions. For instance, the emphasis in the 1980s on strategic business units, business directors, and product-group management grew out of creating organization structures based on the corporate strategy as it is related to specific products and markets. Companies such as Du Pont, IBM, Kodak, and Johnson & Johnson are organized in this manner and are functioning better than before, often in very competitive markets with high volumes of new product introductions.

At one of these firms, management defines the logistics organization based on the needs of the overall business strategy. Specifically, management religiously prepares a mission statement for the business unit, which in turn forms the basis for development of individual product objective statements. These product objectives require logistics to fulfill one of three missions, depending on the business/market situation. The missions read as follows:

A. **Where we have leadership positions...**

- Develop a new aspect of doing business with customers and suppliers every year.

- Implement a major logistics-system change every two years to sustain our lead and avoid complacency.

- Upgrade to next-generation technology every five years.

- Adapt to long-range logistics trends every ten years.

B. **Where we are not number one, but want to be...**

- Identify unfulfilled supplier/customer needs and opportunities.

- Match the logistics curve to product life cycle and major market trends.

- Choose a generic strategy of leadership in either cost, service, quality, or dependability.

- Foster an attitude in logistics of innovating to create new value.

C. **For emerging markets and/or new logistics systems...**

- Create the goal of achieving competitive monopoly.

- Establish pre-emptive logistics systems for rapid exploitation of our competitive advantage.

- Cultivate customers' willingness to pay, i.e., generate strong gross margins.

- Achieve rapid investment payback to finance innovations.

- Know potential logistics technology discontinuities.

This example points out the need to tailor organizational decisions and actions to each unique market segment and strategy.

We must also reflect interdependencies between sales, marketing, operations, and logistics in how we organize. For example, several companies we interviewed had debated whether domestic and international logistics should be separate departments. One factor seemed to drive most of their decisions. It centered around the degree to which domestic and foreign manufacturing and marketing were integrated. If major components and sub-assemblies critical to U.S. operations were produced abroad, close integration of foreign and domestic logistics was essential to a smooth supply chain. If, on the other hand, international markets were sourced from foreign plants, separate departments seemed best for meeting these independent focuses.

By basing its organization structure on changing business/market strategies, and taking the logistics actions necessary to implement these strategies, the company gains the flexibility it needs to compete effectively. As the business strategies change, so too do the organization structures within the firm's business units. This means that reorganizations are not long-term studies; they occur regularly with little pain or fanfare. Every manager is mission- and value-oriented. As a result, this world-class company is highly successful.

CENTRALIZATION VS. DECENTRALIZATION

When discussing organization structure with companies, we frequently are asked, "Should we centralize or decentralize our logistics functions?" Although the issue is valid, the question needs to be more specific. We therefore respond by asking additional questions (note that these questions address the day-to-day management decisions that must be made, not broad functions):

- Who should approve carriers for service?

- Who should select carriers for individual shipments?

- Who should monitor carrier performance?

- Where should freight bills be audited/paid?

As a rule, certain decisions are best made in the field where the applicable physical operations occur. For example, selecting carriers for tomorrow's shipments involves detailed knowledge of specific shipment requirements and of carrier-equipment availability. On the other hand, decisions that require analysis of high-level trade-offs among functions are best made centrally.

When a company decides to rationalize its warehouse network, for instance, it should delegate decision-making authority to an appropriate mix of personnel handling activities (decentralized) and functions (centralized) in the areas of purchasing, transportation, warehousing, customer service, etc. The excellent companies today are creating this mix to enhance logistics' contributions to profitability.

In our studies of logistics departments, we see the following developments on the centralization/decentralization issue:

- Use of more centralized management, linked with corporate restructuring as a result of declining domestic-market growth, economic deflation, or competitive leveraging.

- Creation of comprehensive logistics organizations, with more emphasis on procurement.

- Styling of organizations to support corporate pressures for profit growth through productivity gain and enhanced computer technology.

- Increased emphasis on accountability and functional responsibility.

Although we discuss effective measurements of logistics performance in subsequent chapters, we note here that the organizational units should be focused and measurable. One of the key differences between Japanese and American manufacturers is the former's emphasis on focused organization. Japanese firms measure the success of their teams or groups of people, rather than their individuals. Team performance in achieving targeted results becomes the standard of success--a simple, yet effective, practice.

ACCOUNTABILITY

When reviewing various logistics organization structures, we found it interesting to note how the principle of accountability was applied or avoided. Accountability, as we use the term, refers to an individual's willingness to be measured by results. Being measured by results is the direct opposite of being measured by activity. The latter places value on the **doing** of work rather than on the **results** of work. If the individual is accountable for quality performance and results, and the organization is accountable for meeting employee needs and ensuring economic stability and survival, the entire corporate entity benefits.

Xerox Corporation is a prime example of how the accountability principle works. Xerox issued a challenge to its logistics personnel: "Do you, as an employee of the Xerox logistics division, add value to any Xerox product?"

The company encourages active response to this challenge through its organization set-up. Departmental structure is not based on job descriptions. Rather, it centers around a management approach that encourages individuals to think, create "action plans," and develop "two-person contracts." The latter are agreements between supervisors and their staff as to specific results each employee will strive to achieve and each party's role in accomplishing those goals. They focus on fostering smooth working relationships and support among workers, not on narrow, more traditional, parochial views of productivity. The system also is built around performance evaluations that foster accountability.

This management style could not work without the properly structured logistics organization. Work units are created such that the relationships among Xerox employees encourage the mutual trust and teamwork critical to good performance. For example, one department is responsible for ensuring adequate availability of repair parts to field-service personnel. A broad range of inventory and warehousing functions are assigned directly to this function and other related activities such as parts transportation are closely coordinated with other departments. Over time, people start to challenge their organization as well as their individual work. These methods have propelled logistics to new levels of contribution to profitability--even in the face of increasingly competitive markets.

FOCUS ON THE CUSTOMER

The final element to consider in organizing logistics along strategic lines is customer service. We cannot overemphasize the importance of focusing on the customer at all times. As testimony to our position, all the companies we know of that adhere faithfully to this principle are profitable. In fact, we see a direct correlation between corporate profitability and customer satisfaction. Given this business maxim, isn't it amazing that so few companies organize effectively to ensure customer satisfaction?

In truth, many U.S. manufacturing and merchandising firms have no customer-service organization at all. If a department does exist, it generally handles post-sales service or repair, or answers customer questions through an "800" telephone number.

Companies attempting to justify this absence of service network frequently comment, "Customer service must be an attitude of all our employees. Thus, we do not want an organizational unit with this name or function."

56

We certainly agree that good customer service is an attitude. But why do so few companies deliver it? Why do sales, distribution, production, and other departments rarely agree on how to provide outstanding customer service? Why do most companies neglect to measure it?

The fundamental problems seem to be lack of:

- Focus on the measures of service **that are important to customers**, and

- Clear assignment of primary responsibility for each measure to one organizational unit.

Fortunately, there are notable exceptions to this rule. Companies such as IBM, 3M, Frito-Lay, Caterpillar, and Mars sustain excellence in service, quality, and reliability. Their logistics organizations are driven by customer service, focused on satisfaction, and dedicated to meeting customers' needs. All of these firms are leaders in product quality. Is their preoccupation with customer service, therefore, necessary? Would they be as profitable without fine-tuned service procedures?

To answer such queries, consider the competition these firms face. We work with a conglomerate in which the logistics organization has over three hundred people in its customer-service department. These people-- two-thirds of whom are in field locations--are responsible for order management. This means they manage the processes of entering customer orders, scheduling them through production, and delivering them to the customers. This organization is vested with all authority needed to accomplish these tasks. It exists solely for customer satisfaction, and, as a result, represents a powerful competitive weapon for the conglomerate--a weapon that produces a significant return.

Customer service does not just apply to a company's external customers; it involves internal "clients" as well. A number of businesses are restructuring their operations to reflect this commitment to internal customers. J.C. Penney is a case in point. The retailer's logistics organization has undertaken a two-year project to deliver products internally at service levels comparable to United Parcel Service (UPS), but at much lower cost. This task requires coordination of high-volume delivery for multiple inbound, intracompany, and outbound points. With a clear mission, and top management commitment to high-quality service, however, J.C. Penney's logistics department is meeting its delivery objectives.

ORGANIZATIONS OF THE FUTURE

As we stated earlier, the movement towards comprehensive logistics organizations is gradual and evolutionary. We estimate that only about 5 percent of the **Fortune** 1000 companies are organized so comprehensively (and effectively) that they group all logistics activities under one umbrella and achieve desired levels of accountability and service.

Not long ago, some companies were consumed with cutting costs--to the point that they eliminated staff across the board. As recently as 1983, for instance, a major food-products firm cut its logistics staff so severely that customer service suffered. Although product quality and price were unchanged, clients switched to other suppliers, sales spiraled downward, and the company lost market share.

Fortunately, the firm reversed the trend by setting up "corrective action teams" and implementing other positive turnaround methods designed to re-focus attention on meeting customer needs. Management learned the hard way what can happen when the logistics organization becomes ineffective.

The precise structure of departmental organization does not determine logistics' success within a company. Rather, the way in which logistics activities are managed, perceived, and focused is the key to success. This is why companies preoccupied with organization structure adapt to change so slowly. It also explains why logistics flexibility, i.e., the organizational unit's ability to respond to and implement strategy, can provide a competitive advantage. For this reason, we believe more and more companies will revise the way they structure the logistics organization, giving it the flexibility and responsibility needed to carry out corporate strategy.

Chapter 5
USING THE POWER OF INFORMATION

Few technological advances have affected industry as dramatically as the computer. It is very difficult to pick up an issue of **Business Week, Fortune, Forbes,** or **The Wall Street Journal** and not find an article devoted to some information-system application. Clearly, the dramatic reduction in the cost of obtaining, processing, and transmitting information is changing the way we do business.

More and more, management now views information as a strategic asset. The information systems plan is a strategic plan. This means that companies ascribe strategic value to what essentially is a process. We have always used information to transact business. But, by applying technology in new ways, industry has transformed the process into a "thing." Management is recognizing that the way in which a company uses this "thing" has a considerable impact on the firm's ability to innovate, and its competitive position and profitability.

In this chapter, we focus on the concept of using information as an asset to achieve competitive advantage. Logistics is a transaction-intensive set of functions. Keeping track of the physical activities of logistics, i.e., units handled, stored, shipped, etc., requires computer data-processing capability. What separates world-class logistics organizations from others is their use of information to gain competitive advantage. During our research for this project, we encountered numerous "innovative" logistics information systems and applications.

Because of the rapid rate of change in information technology, companies must constantly develop new systems just to stay even with their competitors. In fact, one vice president of logistics commented to us, "No longer can I let MIS dictate what, how, and when we will get new systems for logistics. We decide for ourselves what we must have, or else we suffer setbacks with our customers."

Information systems, of course, heavily utilize the data-processing speed and capacity of computers. The scope of effective systems, however, transcends electronic technology. One executive, who contributed significantly to our research, describes two aspects of systems:

- "Large S" systems--the complete spectrum of established policies, procedures, decision rules, and operating practices by which we manage our companies.

- "Small S" systems--the integrated hardware/software applications that support and expedite our use of our fundamental large S systems.

We find this distinction insightful. Throughout our research we noted that sound, strategy-focused "large S" systems distinguished companies that gained competitive advantage from information systems from those companies that gained only data-processing efficiency.

In the following paragraphs, we describe instances where information is used in key areas of logistics to strengthen competitive position. We highlight factors companies consider as they combine the "large S" and "small S" aspects of information systems for competitive advantage. We also outline a generalized management-systems planning process that can help a company determine its systems' needs and organize an effective implementation project.

MANUFACTURING AND DISTRIBUTION RESOURCE PLANNING

We found that one of the most popular logistics applications of information technology today is in the planning of a company's manufacturing process and distribution requirements. These programs are referred to as manufacturing resource planning (MRP-II) and distribution resource planning (DRP) systems. MRP-II is designed to help schedule materials, labor, and equipment efficiently; DRP helps plan and manage distribution inventory flows. Both can improve corporate productivity dramatically. In fact, companies successfully implementing MRP-II systems report savings of 25 percent in assembly and indirect-labor costs, 33 percent reductions in inventory investment, and up to 50 percent decreases in overtime costs.

MRP-II's success depends not on the size of the company, but on the effective alignment of the "large S" issues with the MRP-II concept and related software. Advancements in MRP-II systems permit businesses with as few as 50 employees to benefit from their use. As testimony to this statement, we encountered a small manufacturer of industrial products that recouped its investment in MRP-II systems within one year. Today, three years later, the firm is the price leader in its markets because it is the low-cost producer.

MRP-II systems coordinate critical information such as stock location, bills of material, production planning, purchasing, inventory, and costing. In doing so, they help management determine what resources they need to produce the master production schedule. Using this information, management can develop production schedules that reflect what actually can be accomplished. This enables them to make realistic commitments for orders (and forecasts) that accurately reflect materials on hand, raw materials, and manufacturing resources.

The finished-goods distribution counterpart of MRP-II is called distribution resource planning (DRP). DRP programs help coordinate the distribution of finished goods/products from several plant sources through various field-stocking locations. As an on-line, integrated distribution information system, DRP accumulates demands for inventory and other distribution resources "upwards" from the customer to the source plant. It helps plan distribution resources based on forecasts, inventory availability, delivery lead times, and lot sizes. By balancing stocks and shipments, it also helps companies plan supply requirements "downward" from location to location to make the best use of available materials or products.

Several companies indicated they were investing in DRP systems because they expected the payback to be dramatic. Their system requirements analyses called for on-line, real-time systems to enable managers to know exact types and quantities of goods available, where they are located, and probable demand volume and location for those materials. The benefit of this kind of information crosses organizational lines, thereby permitting more integrated operations-management decisions. The information is readily available for reducing inventory and transportation costs, while maintaining high levels of customer service. This means that the return on DRP systems can be very high. As an example, DRP helped achieve the following results for pharmaceuticals manufacturer Abbott Laboratories (Canada):

- Improved customer service performance from an 85 to 97 percent fill rate

- Reduced inventory by 25 percent

- Trimmed distribution costs by 15 percent

- Reduced obsolescence by 80 percent

At Abbott Laboratories, the shift from traditional reaction-to-order-points toward time-phased planning of field-stocking requirements using a DRP system was responsible for these impressive results.

One of the key benefits of DRP systems is that they can be linked directly to MRP systems. In DRP, the distribution requirements end at the master production schedule. In manufacturing, planning requirements begin with the master schedule. The master schedule is "exploded" to establish demands for components and raw materials. By linking MRP and DRP at the master-schedule point, firms are integrating manufacturing and distribution to manage the supply chain more efficiently.

In industries where the logistics function is considered critical to operating success, companies are developing "Computer Integrated Logistics" systems (CILs). Similar in concept to Computer Integrated Manufacturing systems (CIMs), CILs are structured to integrate the key functions of logistics operations, i.e., forecasting, purchasing, transportation, production scheduling, warehousing, inventory management, order processing, and business performance measurement. By integrating these activities, CILs seek to manage the product from raw material to customer delivery.

Although we noted no company with a complete CIL actually in place, we met with several that had targeted them in their long-term systems plans. Their development efforts center around designing and implementing the basic component applications in a staged process. At the same time, they are updating their policies, procedures, and operating practices to take advantage of the new management capabilities CILs provide.

Introduction of advanced information systems such as MRP and DRP does not, by itself, ensure profitability improvements. As with all introductions of new technology, successfully implementing these systems requires companies to also address the changes in operating practices and behavior necessitated by the system. Universally, the executives we interviewed stressed the need to address "large S" aspects of new information systems such as:

- **The closed-loop system.** MRP and DRP systems operate best when feedback to a control mechanism is inherent. Most companies find that operational control in MRP and DRP environments must come from properly trained management. New generations of software are providing more and more control capabilities, but human experience and involvement are still critical.

- **The uniqueness of companies.** All organizations are different. Even though excellent off-the-shelf software packages exist, they must be customized to the particular company for optimum results. Usually modification of **both** the software and company practices simplifies the process and yields the best results.

- **The importance of training.** Personnel require training to be able to use the system to its fullest extent. This training goes beyond how to use the software and encompasses the new operating practices and disciplines inherent in MRP and DRP.

- **Policies, plans, objectives, and priorities.** These systems cannot do everything for everyone, nor can they run themselves. There is no substitute for good systems planning and monitoring that are grounded in the overall logistics strategy. Management must set the policies that will govern how these systems will be used to plan and manage operations.

MRP and DRP systems and their integration can create "information power"--i.e., information used to attain competitive advantage. They help operations managers run their business better than their competitors. Even when competitors have similar systems, each user derives somewhat different efficiency gains. The difference in benefits they derive comes from their rigor in setting policy and their discipline in using the system. Few companies currently realize the full potential of their MRP and DRP systems, because of inadequate attention by senior management to "large S" issues. They still benefit, but they are missing opportunities that could well be captured by increasingly active competitors.

CHANNEL SYSTEMS--ELECTRONIC DATA INTERCHANGE

In Chapter 7 we discuss the principle of excellence that involves creating "win-win" situations through strategic alliances with suppliers and customers. One of the newest targets of opportunity--and one of the largest areas of potential profit enhancement--derives from the use of computer technology to link one company with others in its distribution channel. Known as "channel systems," these computer networks take various forms. Some enable customers to place orders automatically and electronically. Others allow parties to analyze costs, control quality, devise marketing plans, and seek advice electronically. In all cases, companies implementing channel systems use them to increase sales, protect distribution channels, and improve customer service.

American Hospital Supply (AHS) provides an excellent case in point as to the benefits of channel computer systems. In the mid-1970s, AHS installed the industry's first order-taking computer terminals in large hospitals. The company distributes products from some 8,500 manufacturers to more than 100,000 health care providers.

In the ensuing years, AHS grew dramatically to a $3.4 billion-a-year operation. Many attribute this growth to the fact that hospital purchasing agents prefer placing orders on the AHS terminals, and so make larger routine orders. The strategic alliances the system helped foster allowed AHS to cut inventories, improve customer service, and obtain better terms from its suppliers for higher volumes of orders. Without question, this electronic ordering system and the timely, reliable information it generates allow AHS (now part of Baxter Travenol) to stay ahead of its competitors.

Since AHS's innovation, other companies have recorded similar successes in using channel systems. Inland Steel, Eastman Kodak, General Electric, and Reliance Electric, to name a few, have provided order-entry systems to customers and/or distributors. Inland Steel increased its market share over the past few years (the only domestic steelmaker to do so)--a feat many industry observers attribute, in part, to the firm's channel computer system. Customers can enter orders on their Inland Steel terminal, and check shipping dates (customer order status). Inland executives believe the firm's ability to give customers these options, and to ship promptly and reliably, produce inventory savings that more than pay for the computer system. In effect, the terminals help Inland counter the cost advantages of its foreign competitors.

Another channel system with potentially far-reaching implications for the retail food industry is that introduced by General Foods. The company has been testing a system that reads information from bar-code scanners at supermarket checkout counters. The General Foods computer transforms the data by adding economic and demographic information about the store's local marketplace. This analyzed information, in turn, can help the store manager decide what items to stock and promote, and what goods to place on certain shelf locations. Think of the power this information gives General Foods as it becomes the grocery store's market analyst and advisor.

For businesses that market their products through distributors (indirect channels), channel systems offer major opportunities. Most manufacturers want their distributors to be effective and efficient...to add value to their product. Providing distributors with a channel system supports this goal, and commits the company to providing tangible technical assistance that enhances distributor relationships.

The transportation/distribution profession has led the way in advancing the concept of linking systems through electronic data interchange (EDI). During the 1970s, the Transportation Data Coordinating Committee (TDCC) began to solve the technical problems involved in setting standards for the exchange of information between transportation carriers and shippers regarding shipments, bookings, tariffs, etc. Despite slow progress from concept to practice, major advances have been made. In fact, beginning in 1988 Conrail will require all its volume shippers to communicate shipment data in advance via EDI. To encourage early adoption of EDI, they are offering per shipment discounts during 1987.

Today, standards exist to handle data interchange for motor carriers, railroads, grocery, chemical, electrical, and automotive manufacturers, public warehousers, and others. Probably the best-known extension of EDI standards is found in the grocery sector. Called the Uniform Communication Standard (UCS), these protocols for computer-to-computer ordering and similar transactions were adopted early in the 1980s by grocery manufacturers, brokers, distributors, and retailers. Today, no grocery manufacturer can expect to be a major player without using UCS. One large food processor, for example, currently handles over 30 percent of its orders through this medium, and expects this number to increase to over 60 percent within two years.

Not to be outmaneuvered, other transportation organizations have taken steps to automate communications. One such group, the National Customs Brokers and Forwarders Association of America (NCBFAA), reports that almost 300 customs brokers soon will go on-line with the U.S. Customs Service's Automated Broker Interface (ABI) program. These brokers handle nearly 50 percent of imported cargo.

EDI systems such as ABI help reduce the massive amounts of paperwork involved in international trade. We found that even small broker companies are achieving benefits that quickly pay back an investment in this type of computer technology.

Increasingly, logistics professionals refer to EDI within their field as logistics data interchange (LDI). LDI encompasses such applications as:

- Freight payments
- Vendor/purchasing orders
- Transportation ratings and tracking
- Warehouse stocks

- Customer orders

Current data-processing technology permits computer networks to share logistics information among corporate divisions, customers, suppliers, carriers, and others. In addition, the transmission standards exist for public third-party EDI systems that allow small companies to use EDI without making major capital investments.

In short, most of the technical problems associated with EDI have been solved. The corporate logistics executive need only determine what, how, and with whom this mechanism will be used--clearly an area ripe for creative thinking.

DECISION-SUPPORT SYSTEMS

Most "experts" agree that the next wave of computer-systems development--after integrated systems--will be in the area of decision support. Once integrated systems and databases are established for manufacturing and logistics, operations managers will seek ways to make fuller use of the integrated information at their disposal. Enter decision-support systems (DSS).

When we refer to DSS, we speak about software that supports managers in making strategic or operational decisions about their businesses. DSS differ from traditional transaction-processing systems, which handle repetitive operations. DSS are designed to analyze and evaluate the major quantitative and qualitative factors that routinely influence management decisions. In practical logistics applications to date DSS focus on quantifying the cost and service implications of operating alternatives--for example, shipping direct from manufacturing plants to customers versus using field warehouses or distribution centers. Companies are finding that DSS applications allow decision makers to quickly consider a range of factors and options that are inconceivable to address without computer aid. The cost and service effectiveness of their decisions improves measurably as a result.

A new category of DSS--encompassing artificial intelligence (AI) and expert systems--is under development at some pioneering companies. Broadly speaking, they are computer systems that perform at the level of intelligent human behavior, simulating the reasoning processes humans might use to solve a problem. Expert systems, for example, can offer access to information not readily available within a company, e.g., a database containing the knowledge of specialists in an area such as transportation.

These systems draw inferences based on facts input into them and decision rules that are programmed in special A.I. languages or in conventional ones such as COBOL.

How can DSS be used in a logistics environment? Let's consider some examples. Earlier we discussed MRP and DRP systems as useful tools with which to plan and monitor production and distribution operations. While these systems are good at monitoring and tracking materials and inventory, they are limited in their capacity to help managers decide questions such as:

- Where should a given order/product be produced?

- Where should we stock the finished goods?

- From which stocking location should an order be shipped?

- How should we adapt to changing customer orders or preferences (i.e., terms, volumes, etc.)?

Discussing these questions recently, a president of an electronics corporation explained that the company had installed MRP and DRP systems some three years ago. Although management was satisfied with the systems' performance and resulting improvements in operations, the president was frustrated because the systems could not address the kinds of questions listed above. Thus, while the executive believed the firm's processes for monitoring, tracking, and planning for materials and inventories were adequate, he thought the important decisions of "where, what, and why" were not being reached in the best manner.

A new approach is being developed to enhance MRP and DRP systems with these kinds of decision-making capabilities. It is referred to as **Demand Management**. Basically, it includes decision-support software that enables logistics managers to decide where to produce and distribute from on a dynamic basis, considering product demand, production capacities, costs, and service levels.

The recent experience of a national consumer-products company that has multiple plants, product lines, and stocking locations illustrates the benefits. A demand management application was developed that enabled them to automate a previously manual and highly judgmental process of allocating sales demand to plants. The result was lower costs, better service, and improved profits.

Another example of where a customized DSS approach is appropriate is in the warehouse or distribution center. While several commercially available warehouse information systems provide the ability to track where product is stored within the warehouse, none really help managers decide where within the facility a product group or stockkeeping unit (SKU) should be stored. That capability helps the few companies that have it fine-tune their operations to significantly improve asset utilization and labor productivity.

EVOLVING LOGISTICS SYSTEMS

The rapid evolution of computer technology, together with the proliferation of packaged software programs and their marketing "hype," have done nothing but confuse business managers. Repeatedly, we are asked by logistics, financial, and other executives what kinds of logistics systems make sense in today's business environment. These questions usually take the following forms:

- How can we decide what our company really needs or should do?

- How should we assess the costs and benefits of logistics information systems?

- How can we evaluate either our staffs' proposals for systems or outside software vendors' claims and proposals?

- How "good" are the available DRP and MRP systems?

- Is it really possible to implement integrated logistics systems?

- What are the policy and management actions that are needed to support our systems strategy?

Although detailed answers to these queries would take us beyond the scope of this report, from our research and experience we can offer some general guidelines to executives faced with these questions. Many companies are using a multi-step approach to evaluating, planning, and implementing logistics-processing systems. The overall purpose of this approach is to answer these questions as they relate to the company's logistics operations: What is going on today? What problems (or missed opportunities) are created by the current approach? What should we be doing?

Companies use different approaches to addressing these issues but they have common needs. Their system-planning process must reflect the strategies, policies, and business needs of the company's logistics operations. Furthermore, it must address what manual and computerized information systems should be developed, and why. For this reason, several successful companies follow a process called Logistics Systems Planning (LSP). This process focuses on the company's **business** and **logistics needs**, rather than on the computer. The LSP approach looks like this:

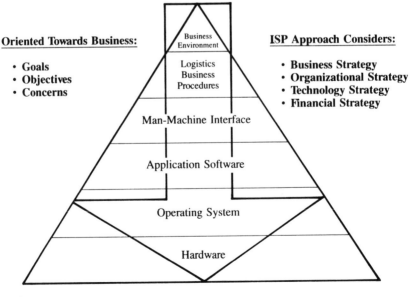

In this process companies start with the business environment and identify the strategic and competitive requirements for their systems. They next identify the requirements dictated by their current or desired logistics business procedures. They also specifically address how their people and systems will interface. Only then do they probe the software and hardware requirements that have been the primary focus of traditional systems planning processes. We found that most companies with effective logistics systems follow steps of this type in their planning.

Another way to view this process is illustrated on the next page. Notice that this type of systems planning approach is characterized by certain key features:

- The process is initiated with a substantive review of business strategy, operations, and current systems.

- Short-term improvements are identified early, so the system does not require years to yield results.

- High-level designs and requirements are addressed first.

- Plans are developed for applications, technology, and organizational changes.

- Projects are prepared to carry out the work.

The Logistics Systems Planning Process
Conceptual Overview

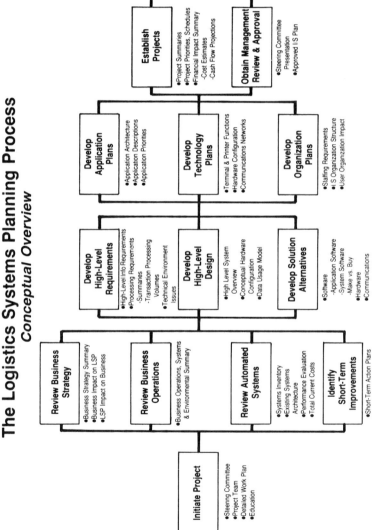

Initiate Project
- Steering Committee
- Project Team
- Detailed Work Plan
- Education

Review Business Strategy
- Business Strategy Summary
- Business Impact on LSP
- LSP Impact on Business

Review Business Operations
- Business Operations, Systems & Environmental Summary

Review Automated Systems
- Systems Inventory
- Existing Systems Architecture
- Performance Evaluation
- Total Current Costs

Identify Short-Term Improvements
- Short-Term Action Plans

Develop High-Level Requirements
- High-Level Info Requirements
- Processing Requirements
  - Summaries
  - Transaction Processing Volumes
- Technical Environment Issues

Develop High-Level Design
- High Level System Overview
- Conceptual Hardware Configuration
- Data Usage Model

Develop Solution Alternatives
- Software
  - Application Software
  - System Software
  - Make vs. Buy
- Hardware
- Communications

Develop Application Plans
- Application Architecture
- Application Descriptions
- Application Priorities

Develop Technology Plans
- Terminal & Printer Functions
- Hardware Configuration
- Communications Networks

Develop Organization Plans
- Staffing Requirements
- I/S Organization Structure
- User Organization Impact

Establish Projects
- Project Summaries
- Project Priorities, Schedules
- Financial Impact Summary
  - Cost Estimates
  - Cash Flow Projections

Obtain Management Review & Approval
- Steering Committee Presentation
- Approved I/S Plan

Most of the logistics systems described were designed and implemented by following similar approaches. The specific method used should be tailored to the individual company's situation, of course. Success, however, depends most on getting broad-based, senior-level support for the planning effort. The experience of one leading consumer-goods manufacturer illustrates this point. This manufacturer established the planning project at the senior operations-management level. The firm organized an implementation steering committee consisting of the vice-presidents of logistics, production, sales and marketing, finance, MIS, and purchasing. These committee members functioned as directors of the effort, reviewing progress, plans, and recommended projects. The team followed a structured LSP approach to the letter and, in a matter of months, produced a solid plan for upgrading the company's logistics systems. Functional integration and an organized planning approach, as this company found, are the keys to developing effective logistics systems.

FUTURE INFORMATION TRENDS

We mentioned earlier that viewing information as an asset gives strategic importance to the "thing" called information systems. We also noted that the rate of change in information technology and applications is escalating rapidly.

What kinds of changes are likely to occur in the logistics systems area? Based on contact with logistics and MIS executives, with executives of leading software firms, and through Ernst & Whinney's network of manufacturing, logistics, and information-systems resources, we believe the following trends will shape the logistics systems of the future.

Systems integration. Business will see increased functional integration among logistics, manufacturing, finance, sales, marketing, and other operating units. Computer systems designs will reflect this integration as well. Already, a number of companies are working toward this goal, and software developers are designing systems to meet the needs of fully integrated organizations.

Systems comprehensiveness. As information technology evolves, and the speed of data processing accelerates, systems will become broader in scope and depth. The "disaggregation" of data and transactions down to the lowest level of detail will become more prevalent. This also means that the availability of the detailed data necessary for day-to-day logistics operations decisions will increase.

Specific applications. The number of specific software applications--primarily microcomputer-based--will increase. One executive asked us if software comprehensiveness and applications specificity were not contradictory terms. We do not believe so. It is entirely possible (and indeed likely) that mini- and mainframe computer systems will become more comprehensive in scope, while microcomputers will become more functional in application. The latter probably will occur in microcomputers interfacing with large databases as well as with microcomputer-specific applications.

EDI. As we suggested earlier in this chapter, the partnership opportunities associated with Electronic Data Interchange and channel systems appear unlimited. In Chapter 7, we discuss the business benefits of "strategic alliances." By providing the information link among business partners, EDI will supply a critical element for these alliances.

Most of the technical problems associated with EDI have been solved. The opportunity, therefore, lies in electronically linking the different parties in the value chain--suppliers, manufacturers/producers, distributors, and customers. Such linkages are perfectly suited to Just-in-Time operations, for example.

These facts were emphasized clearly at the 1986 annual conference of the Transportation Data Coordinating Committee. The meeting focused on EDI applications and opportunities in more than a dozen specific industries. The breadth of the TDCC conference and its record attendance in 1986 (1,500 people) mark the beginning of a new era of data exchange for mutual benefit among separate organizations. We expect these data systems to have a positive effect on logistics' contribution to corporate profitability.

Value-Added Networks (VANs). In addition to EDI, another type of information-exchange system--the value-added network--is emerging in business. In basic form a VAN consists of three parts: a mainframe computer at a central location; digital switches and transmission equipment that route data through a fiber-optic cable, over a wire, or by satellite to computers in remote locations; and software to operate the system. As with EDI, applications are limited only by managers' imagination. In the logistics area, we have come across several VAN projects that are especially interesting:

- General Motors and other automakers are working on systems to permit customers and dealers to order a car electronically. The vehicle will be built and delivered within a brief time period.

- Large transportation companies (mostly motor carriers) use VANs to track shipments, equipment, and related operations.

- Retailers, manufacturers, and distributors in consumer products use VANs to manage products from the raw materials stage to the checkout counter.

As with other similar information systems, the return on investment with a VAN may not be readily or immediately identifiable. In fact, VANs may be "loss leaders" initially. Based on the successful use of VANs at certain firms, however, we believe they clearly represent a potential tool for gaining competitive advantage.

DSS. As we noted earlier in our discussion of decision-support systems, we see these programs becoming valuable resources for the logistics manager. They will help logistics executives make business decisions faster and better than their competitors.

Admittedly, this chapter only "scratches the surface" with regard to the future of information technology in U.S. industry and in logistics. Companies are just beginning to exploit the considerable opportunities that information systems offer. Management is still in the first stages of learning to handle information as a business asset. Corporate culture in this area is changing fast, however, and we expect the pace of innovation and implementation to pick up.

Given this scenario, logistics executives nevertheless must continue to focus on the real business purpose of information technology. A logistics vice president of a large manufacturer succinctly defined this purpose for us: "Our goal, similar to the logistics objectives with our products, is to get the right information to the right person at the right time, so that the right decision can be made for the right reason--to beat our competitors."

It is interesting to note that, for over twenty years, the logistics profession has been trying to get the right **product** to the right place at the right time. Now--in the mid-1980s and beyond--we strive for excellence (and competitive advantage) by "substituting information for inventory." The companies that learn to do this well, while also getting the right products distributed properly, will be the winners in tomorrow's marketplace.

Chapter 6
EMPHASIZING HUMAN RESOURCES

While conducting the research for this book, we were surprised by the frequency with which executives stressed the importance of human resources to corporate profitability. Frequently, these managers ranked high-quality people as their most important asset. They further stated that without effective, loyal personnel, the logistics function could not contribute to corporate profitability.

In his book, **What They Don't Teach You At Harvard Business School**, Mark McCormack offers the following comments on the importance of effective human-resource management:

> *"I can't imagine anyone being effective in business without having some insight into people. Business itself is such a subtle matter of taking a slight edge here, an imperceptible edge there. And every aspect of the process comes back to people--managing them, selling them, working with them, simply getting them to do what you want them to do. Without insight there is no subtlety...."* [8]

Unfortunately, we have seen too many situations where employees are undervalued or treated improperly. In many cases, corporate executives understand the value of effectively managed people, but fail to act on their beliefs.

The public, whether customers, shareholders, suppliers, or channel partners, tends to base its opinions about a company on its perception of how the firm treats its people and customers. Because logistics crosses organizational lines and interacts heavily with suppliers and customers, it plays as important a role in shaping this corporate image as do sales and marketing people. Top management often overlooks this fact--to the detriment of the company. As one logistics executive pointed out, "Our people are the last ones in the company to interact with customers on their orders. The impressions (both good and bad) they make can last a long time!"

To complement the organization principle outlined in Chapter 4, and to highlight what factors are important in contributing to corporate profitability, we devote this chapter to a discussion of how leading logistics organizations treat their people. The guidelines these firms employ are based on the belief that logistics excellence can only be achieved through people.

STANDARDS OF QUALITY

In discussing our 10 principles of logistics excellence with a number of executives, we were asked whether "quality" shouldn't be added as an eleventh principle. We opted against this suggestion because quality is not a unique activity. It is achieved through the intelligent application of these principles. Many executives we interviewed stressed that quality is inherent in each of the principles as the factor that separates average companies from the best. It is not enough to practice the principles; the best logistics organizations instill and sustain a high level of quality behavior day by day.

Quality and human resources are inextricably linked. If you do not instill a quality orientation into your people, nothing else will be really successful in achieving quality products and services. The most profitable companies manage their logistics people in such a way as to make quality a daily priority. One company that sustains such quality in logistics is retailer L.L. Bean of Freeport, Maine. This firm was started in 1912 and now records sales of $335 million. Eighty-five percent of L.L. Bean's business is handled through mail orders. The company distributes some 70 million catalogues a year which list over 3,000 items. Twice this many products are available at the Maine retail store. About 20 percent of sales are for products the company manufactures itself. L.L. Bean prides itself on a quality of logistics performance that most companies may never attain. For example, the company reports a correct order-fill rate of 99.89 percent. With almost six million orders handled annually, this rate is phenomenal!

Does the company rely on computers to achieve this kind of quality? Yes and no. Obviously, L.L. Bean's transaction volume requires sizeable information-processing capability. And, the retailer recently invested in some decision-support software for packing and shipping applications. Without computers, the company could not effectively handle its present order volume.

More important to the retailer's success, however, are its employees. They work in full concert with computers. In fact, the L.L. Bean warehouse system design was chosen with the full participation of the hourly work force. Created in the 1970s, this warehouse system was thought to be the first of its kind designed by quality circles. It incorporated automated storage and retrieval equipment into the system design chosen by the workers. The computer directs such warehousing activities as locating products, scheduling order fill, measuring productivity, and monitoring shipments.

L.L. Bean employs some 1,800 permanent and 200 temporary workers. Most come from the Maine area and enjoy the outdoors, the company's merchandise, and serving customers. All newly hired employees go through an extensive training/re-training program, designed to educate them as to the firm's quality standards. Workers soon learn that these standards motivate, support, and reward high-quality performance. Thus, the company derives its success not only from the products it sells, but from the people who deliver them.

The fundamental orientation toward quality exhibited by L.L. Bean is one of the keys to the company's financial success. Although the benefits of this approach seem obvious, we found that many companies had trouble achieving this type of orientation. The "father" of statistical process control, W. Edwards Deming, has argued that most U.S. managers do not know how to manage for quality and consistent performance improvement. He contends that management still does not understand the difference between price and value. Rather than providing high customer value through quality, American managers strive to maximize profits by stimulating demand through price concessions. In the current competitive, low-growth global economy, Mr. Deming believes such a policy can be disastrous.

In general, we agree with Mr. Deming's conclusions concerning inadequate attention to quality in U.S. companies. There are many exceptions, however, where the people involved in well-managed logistics organizations are meeting quality challenges. One such example is Pfizer, Inc., a $3.8 billion manufacturer, marketer, and distributor of pharmaceuticals, agricultural, specialty-chemical, and consumer products. At Pfizer, quality-conscious people work together with sophisticated computer systems to provide top-notch customer service. Like many large companies, Pfizer's corporate logistics functions sell their services to other divisions. This practice encourages logistics managers to track costs and productivity rates carefully, and maintain high standards of performance.

Continuous measurement of logistics performance, however, does not guarantee logistics quality. Only people can create that. So, Pfizer involves its logistics personnel in defining and refining their department's performance-measurement system. In fact, many facets of the Pfizer performance-measurement system evolved out of employee suggestions. The system measures warehouse productivity rates, labor usage for distribution services, customer-service transactions per hour, as well as errors per thousand line items processed. The last item is particularly interesting, because it helps the distribution staff catch and correct errors made by others involved in serving customers such as carriers, and sales and production. This saves Pfizer money. As the company's vice president of distribution said, "An error can cost us three to four times more to correct than to do it right the first time. This is why our logistics people are so important."

Pillsbury Company, the grocery-products giant, is another example of a company that has successfully linked quality-performance standards to operations. Pillsbury implemented a warehouse productivity measurement system that aids operations planning and scheduling as well as monitoring labor performance. A central feature of Pillsbury's approach is the ability to identify, by activity, where employees are performing well and where they need help. Top performers of key activities are recognized and encouraged to help the other employees adopt their effective techniques.

This approach has fostered better team work and has significantly improved the quality of warehouse operations and responsiveness to customers. The additional business and reduced costs that have resulted have made a marked contribution to Pillsbury's profitability.

HUMAN RESOURCE MANAGERS

In one of its 1986 issues, **Business Week** published an article entitled "Business Fads: What's In and What's Out." Among the "in" fads, the magazine listed "touchy-feely managers." In a somewhat tongue-in-cheek vein, the article described these managers as "nice-guy bosses who are laying off still more workers."

The writer's wit notwithstanding, we agree that the "touchy-feely" management style is in, but disagree that it is used only to "reduce head-count." Unquestionably, companies have been trimming staffs in order to become more cost-competitive. At the same time, however, they are working to manage their human resources as investments. This approach makes sense in light of the time and money companies spend on their people in hiring, training, evaluating, and developing them.

The emergence of human-resource managers is a welcome develop-ment in the **Fortune** 1000 companies. Managers who deal with the "people" issues in the company--hiring, firing, promotion, pay, benefits, discipline, training, and union relations--are gaining power and influence. Whether the department performing these functions is called personnel, industrial rela-tions, or human resources, the importance of its business mission soon will equal that of sales, marketing, finance, or logistics. We find well-known companies like General Electric, IBM, General Motors, Ford, TRW, and GTE leading the field in elevating the human-resource position to a strategic level.

One of the catalysts driving this trend is the increasing frequency of mergers, acquisitions, division spin-offs, new business ventures, and the like. The accelerated rate at which strategic decisions occur in this environment of change has pinpointed the need to match skills with jobs, retain key people, and solve human problems that arise from new technology, products, and lines of business.

Historically, many companies' approaches to managing logistics opera-tions have evolved over years of trial and error experimentation. Top logis-tics managers were those with extensive experience and historical perspec-tive. Now the highly dynamic environment logistics managers face calls for a different orientation. Innovation and creativity are critical. The ability to communicate and negotiate using new information technologies and automated analysis tools was frequently cited to us as a factor that differentiates successful logistics managers today.

At the same time, top management is realizing that good people help give organizations a competitive edge. At IBM, for example, strategic planning is closely aligned to human-resource management at plant, division, and corporate levels. IBM human-resource managers develop five-year strategic plans in the spring and two-year tactical plans in the fall. All major business decisions are routed through the chief personnel officer. To preserve IBM's policy of no layoffs, human-resource managers maintain rosters of employees' occupational skills. Using these rosters, they plan the redeployment of people from shrinking businesses to growing ones. IBM applied this practice with employees when shutting down a Midwest distribution center. Hundreds of employees were offered new jobs elsewhere in the company. This helped maintain the jobs of valuable employees, but also expanded the distribution and customer-service awareness in the departments these employees joined.

In companies that don't follow these practices on the personnel-department level, we see cases where individual logistics departments set up their own human-resource manager to act as a liaison with the firm's overall personnel function. This practice helps logistics departments attract people who can adapt readily to a dynamic environment that requires coordination of activities with other corporate departments. It also ensures that people with the right skills are recognized and given appropriate opportunities for career advancement.

At one multi-billion-dollar manufacturer, the logistics department requires each headquarters and field manager to submit information on their top two employees. They summarize the individual's strengths, weaknesses, and career objectives. The company has been drawing upon this "talent pool" to fill key management openings and to upgrade the quality of its logistics operations.

TRAINING, MORE TRAINING, AND RE-TRAINING

Many executives we interviewed believe managers should embrace change as a positive entity, and constantly ask themselves, "What have we changed lately?" They argue that traditional practices of challenging sales levels, project schedules, and budget variances are outdated. They are the wrong questions to ask in today's business environment.

The logic of this argument is hard to dispute, given the current competitive business environment. New competitors, business arrangements, products, and technologies are entering our industries more rapidly than ever. Clearly, change is becoming a routine element in business. The manager is becoming a manager of change. He or she will have to make decisions and take action at an unprecedented rate. Survival of the business depends on it.

As a direct result of this environment of change, the need for training or re-training has never been more pressing. Unfortunately, this need often is overlooked--not because firms don't believe in training or don't realize its importance. Rather, these companies treat training as a discretionary budget item that receives funding in good years, and no funding in off years. Management at these firms views training as an option, not as a strategic **need**.

When we asked about their training expenditures, a surprising number of executives admitted that training funds as a percentage of their total budgets varied a great deal from year to year. They believed that in some years "they just couldn't afford training."

Certainly not everyone felt this way. One major electronics firm attributes its perennial market leadership, in part, to its highly trained labor force. This firm keeps its employees on the "cutting edge" of logistics techniques and completely briefed on its new products and marketing initiatives. To them, this is as critical to their long-term financial success as developing new technologies and products.

We believe their view is widely applicable. We noted a number of cases where strategic initiatives were stymied or delayed due to inadequate attention to employee training. New-product introductions that make necessary unique distribution support, combination of multi-division business at distribution centers, and adoption of new electronic order-processing technology are a few of the new developments we have seen companies undertake without adequately orienting the employees that were key to the initiatives' success. In some cases, customer relations disasters resulted. For the fortunate companies, successful implementation was merely delayed. Making sure that employees **know** what we want them to do is so very basic that it is easy to overlook.

In the best logistics organizations, management complements on-the-job training with outside educational programs. These programs range from generalized subjects such as time management to logistics-management updates, such as the logistics seminars held at leading universities. These companies also sponsor focused in-house classes and workshops aimed at informing people of new technologies or business ventures, or other types of imminent change. In anticipation of a major computer-systems overhaul, a leading food company held six all-day workshops on effective logistics practices for dozens of its operations managers. This approach is gaining popularity because of its focus on company-specific operations. Unlike outside multi-company seminars where participants are reluctant to share competitive secrets or specific company problems, the focused in-house workshops can effect change because they target the unique actions that each logistics manager must take.

In another case, a consumer-products manufacturer embarked on a major quality effort and enrolled hundreds of employees in training programs tailored to company needs. The approach focused on education needs at several levels. All affected employees were initially trained in the quality concepts they wished to adopt. Subsequent training was tailored for various employee groups. Senior management was instructed on supplier, customer, and interdepartmental issues. Field logistics employees were trained in unique techniques for their functional responsibilities. Eventually even outside supplier and carrier training was conducted. The company has attributed much of the success of its quality program to this early training and to the employee knowledge and support it fostered.

For the logistics function of today and tomorrow, change is a way of life. Inability to handle change may cost a firm customers and market share.

This is why an ongoing training effort is so important. It helps people adapt quickly to their changing environment and work more efficiently as a result. In addition, ongoing training cuts time required for companies to adjust to changes and speeds the payback period for planned changes.

LOGISTICS PRODUCTIVITY--ITS IMPACTS

Labor productivity has been a hot topic in business circles for many years. In the distribution area, productivity was the subject of two major research projects sponsored by the Council of Logistics Management. These writings referred to the cost-savings opportunities in logistics as a "$40 billion gold mine." Hundreds of companies, as a result, have instituted logistics productivity-improvement programs. Few, however, have achieved "Class IV," or the highest level of efficiency, in their distribution operations.

Productivity improvement is an ongoing goal of the best logistics organizations. As a result, management at these firms is always on the lookout for ways to renew emphasis on productivity and to achieve further gains. For example, a major grocery-products manufacturer transformed its East Coast distribution center into an effective profitability-improvement tool by emphasizing "people programs." Rather than spend money on sophisticated equipment, the company adopted programs designed to improve employee morale and motivation and to promote more efficient warehousing techniques. Groups similar to quality circles were created. These groups continued to meet for a period of two years. Additionally, employee training programs were initiated and conducted on an ongoing basis. People, not machines, were the focus of management attention.

The program generated impressive results. First, labor productivity rose. Unnecessary and redundant procedures were eliminated, thereby saving time and money. The center handled more volume in less time, with half the number of people!

The program produced additional, somewhat unexpected results. As productivity improved, so too did service. Fewer shipment errors were made, delivery lead times were reduced, and customer orders were handled with enthusiasm and accuracy. The system fostered tighter linkages with the sales/marketing and production departments. Unexpectedly, sales from this distribution center increased.

When the company was acquired by a large U.S. corporation, the new top management recognized immediately that the people programs at this distribution center were special. So, management expanded the project corporate-wide. In doing so, management acknowledged the difference that quality distribution people could make to corporate profitability.

Business author Peter Drucker has stated that measuring and improving white-collar productivity is an untapped opportunity. He refutes the contention that this element of business is unmeasurable. He emphasizes that the key to improving a department's effectiveness is not to merely measure activity levels, but to focus on the department's contribution to the company's overall objectives. Drucker's approach calls for specifying contributions to be made by the department and its employees **and** for measuring **results**.

With some fine-tuning, these measures can be applied to logistics personnel. In such cases, logistics people should ask themselves, "What should we be doing for profitability? How should we measure our value to products? How can we achieve higher levels of customer service at lower costs?"

Defining logistics productivity in customer terms, and committing to quality service, can add real meaning to the phrase "people are our most important asset." The best logistics organizations achieve and sustain profitability by managing their personnel as a valuable corporate asset.

Chapter 7
FORMING STRATEGIC ALLIANCES

Stiff competition from Japanese manufacturers has forced the American business community to take a hard look at the way firms in the two countries do business. A study of Japanese business practices reveals several intriguing contrasts. At the top of this list is the fact that the Japanese don't "do" business with their supply/demand-chain partners. Rather, they commit to a business-partner relationship that is presumed to be long-lasting, if not permanent. No matter how good the supplier's products or services are, or how low the price, the involved parties have no relationship until they commit to a binding business partnership.

These "win-win" partnerships do not arise simply for cultural reasons. Rather, they generate the kind of strategic and operational value that produces long-term gains for both parties. Successful operating practices such as Just-in-Time manufacturing have evolved from these partnerships.

U.S. companies that do well in Japan--Coca-Cola, Johnson & Johnson, Schick, Hewlett-Packard, and Xerox--are those that form effective partnerships. These partnerships are based, first and foremost, on shared corporate values and strategic goals. In addition, they rely on close communication and coordination of plans and activities, to the point of sharing plans for new products or market expansions.

Congruence of strategies and sharing of plans are critical, but effective alliances must extend to operational coordination as well. For example, in Chapter 6, we described some of the advantages of using electronic data interchange among product-chain partners. Electronic information-sharing is an excellent way to coordinate operations and sustain strategic partnerships. Other methods are available as well. We describe several in this chapter.

Also in this section, we discuss the rationale for forming strategic alliances, provide case examples of successful partnerships, and offer suggestions on starting up or enhancing such relationships. We believe that, in coming years, world-class organizations will enter into more and more strategic alliances as a means of enhancing profitability--logistics is a key to this process.

INDUSTRY-SPECIFIC VALUE CHAINS

Returning briefly to the value-chain concept, we begin to see how coordinated value-added activities can impact each party in the chain. Clearly, linkages exist not only within the company's internal value chain, but also between the firm's internal chain and those of its suppliers, channel members, and customers. The quality of the channel members' business performance affects the customer's perception of value received and ultimately the profitability of everyone in the chain. For example, a supplier agreeing to ship in more frequent, smaller lots can reduce its customer's inventory. Or, a supplier commitment to use custom packaging for the buyer's products can reduce the latter's inbound-materials inspection costs. This broad view of channel profitability must be adopted to make strategic alliances successful.

Channel-member linkages can and should create value. Product costs reflect the value/costs added by each partner to a product as it moves through the value chain. Thus, the actions of every value-chain member impact a product's end price and perceived value. These interactive relationships among business partners stress the need for setting common strategies and plans before beginning operational execution.

In the exhibit on the next page, we illustrate an example of such a comprehensively linked value chain found in the food industry. The grocery-products sector is familiar to most people because of its obvious consumer orientation. Large food processors, such as Nabisco, General Foods, and Ralston Purina, operate within hundreds of value chains because of their vast number of products, business units, suppliers, and channel members. The president of one of the largest grocery-products corporations told us that one of the firm's major strategic goals is to manage products "from the grain fields to the pantry." This statement reflects top management's "global" view of logistics as a value chain that encompasses every step of product life cycle, from raw materials to finished goods. It also implies a belief that the company can achieve real strategic and competitive advantage by managing the value chains of all parties in the pipeline. Indeed, this is **integrated logistics management** in its most profitable form.

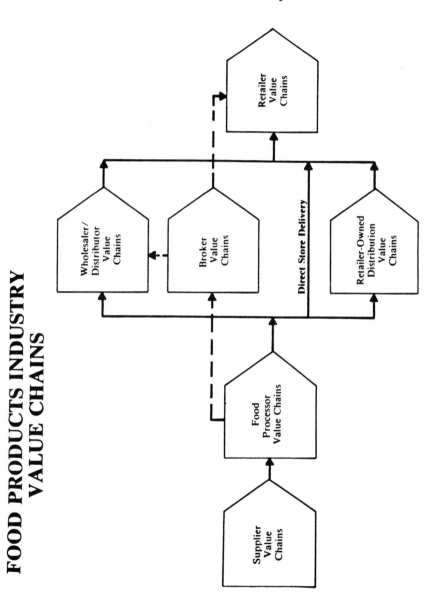

FOOD PRODUCTS INDUSTRY VALUE CHAINS

As corporations or business units consider their relationships with trading partners, they need to assess the quality of their value-chain linkages. This assessment should focus on **all** points of mutual interaction, e.g., order entry and delivery, sales, finance, customer service, joint proposals, and the like. The number of interaction points identified by such a study often surprises executives. Frequently, management assumes that interaction occurs solely during actual business transactions.

Effectively managing these interaction points can make a big difference to a firm. As proof of this statement, we cite General Electric's practice of having field representatives visit distributors weekly to see if "everything is going well." These representatives have the authority to evaluate all aspects of a given partnership--from inventory levels to promotions--and institute corrections as appropriate. This cross-functional review of the respective business partners' value chains helps guarantee that these alliances provide maximum competitive advantage for those involved.

RE-THINKING DISTRIBUTION CHANNELS

As competitive and cost pressures intensify and the number and types of alternative channels increase, we see companies re-thinking how they get their products to market. Management is finding that choosing the right mix of methods, and achieving the right strategic alliances, is a complex, critical task. It also is a never-ending job in most industries.

The need to re-think product pipelines raises the question, "How can we refine our channels on an ongoing basis and still maintain long-term partnerships?" This issue explains why we should select partners who will agree to evolve with us to capitalize on a major market or business concept. This "strategic commitment" is ultimately more important to an effective alliance than an initial, superficial business fit. When partners have aligned their fundamental strategies, they avoid "directional issues" each time there is a market force change. Thus, they do not debate direction. If truly committed, they just focus on doing what is necessary to advance their joint business position.

In addition to these basic strategy considerations, there are other issues of importance to structuring strategic alliances. Management should also consider the kinds of distribution-channel options available. These options generally fall under the headings of **direct** and **indirect** channels. As outlined below, certain basic components comprise the two types of channels:

Direct Channels

- Company sales force (specialists or generalists)
- Company agents (representatives, agents, brokers, merchants, telemarketers)
- Company-owned retail outlets
- Company-owned wholesale outlets
- Company-owned distribution centers
- Company-owned warehouses or other stocking locations

Indirect Channels

- Wholesalers
- Industrial retailers
- Independent retailers
- Franchise outlets
- Public warehouses
- Third-party distributors
- Drop shippers
- Other arrangements

Most organizational arrangements fall within these categories, but variations within each group can be appreciable. For example, the medical-products industry, which supplies a broad range of items to thousands of hospitals, physicians, nursing homes, home-care points, and other health care sites, is undergoing major reorganization. This restructuring stems from several developments, including implementation of new distribution arrangements which involve innovative mixes of direct and indirect channels. It was prompted by the unprecedented public pressure for health care cost containment.

For example, Voluntary Hospitals of America (VHA), a chain of hospitals nationwide, recently created VHA Supply Company (VHASC) to reduce costs and improve medical-product distribution. VHASC is comprised of a network of nine independent regional distributors who have joined VHA in this venture. By combining the purchase volumes of its member hospitals and the specialized technical and distribution expertise of the distributors, VHA is offering its hospitals streamlined pricing structures, reduced cost, **and** more responsive service. In turn, each of the distributors has gained a greater share of the VHA volume in its region--clearly, a "win-win" situation.

As another example of a major distribution channel overhaul, a large electronics manufacturer recently converted from direct distribution to customers to distributing through 75 industrial distributors. The objective of the change-over was to establish close partnerships with a group of top-quality distributors who have established special relationships within the company's industrial customers. The firm's high-tech product, used in industrial automation, requires technical sales, service, and support engineers. The manufacturer intensified its training and support programs, focusing heavily on the new partnerships with distributors. It is now responsible for training and updating over a thousand sales engineers in the unique features of its products. Obviously, managing such an expanded distribution channel requires constant analysis and evaluation on the company's part. The initial results, however, are making the effort worthwhile. Lagging sales have increased markedly, customer satisfaction and referrals are up, and post-sales service costs have decreased due to better matching of their products with customer needs.

Perhaps the most widely known example of channel conversion is that conducted by IBM to manage the introduction of its personal computer

(PC) product line. Prior to introducing the PC in 1981, virtually all of IBM's products were sold direct to customers. For the PC, however, IBM devised a strategy that involved dealing directly with large customers and serving small customers through independent dealers. This strategy enabled the company to reach a broader marketplace--key to achieving the sales volumes necessary for the low per-unit costs sought. By introducing the product in both channels simultaneously, IBM signalled an equal commitment to both forms of distribution.

Occasional conflicts did arise when the two IBM channels competed for the same customer. Nevertheless, the IBM-dealer strategic alliance survived these difficulties. It evolved into a strong dealer network characterized by a high degree of specialization into specific product segments, i.e., multiuser systems, networking services, etc. Indeed, IBM is a pioneer in Value-Added Remarketer (distributor) programs and continued commitment to indirect distribution channels. These alliances were a major reason why IBM gained a far greater market share than competitors with technologically superior products.

JIT SUPPLY AND DELIVERY

Perhaps the greatest opportunity for demonstrating the sustaining value of strategic alliances lies in "Just-in-Time logistics," or supply and delivery operations. In many companies we interviewed, the adoption of JIT concepts heavily emphasized shop-floor issues such as cellular manufacturing and set-up reductions. Their efforts in these areas provided measurable improvements but they are realizing that there are a whole series of other important issues outside the four walls of their plants. In spite of their improvements in manufacturing operations, suppliers and customers operate independently interacting only on individual orders. Each party carries "buffer" inventory that protects against wide fluctuations in demand or failure to deliver ordered goods. Thus, stock duplication continues throughout the value chain.

Furthermore, the customer, hoping to take advantage of the lower-cost, larger-delivery sizes, orders infrequently, thereby requiring more safety stocks. Similarly, the supplier produces infrequently, so must maintain high stocks as well. This duplication is costly and inefficient.

The solution to this scenario lies in creating JIT partnerships among value-chain suppliers and customers. These partnerships require the close cooperation of all parties in order to eliminate double buffers, provide frequent deliveries, establish long-term arrangements, and realize the market benefits of better service.

Elimination of buffer stocks throughout the pipeline means suppliers, vendors, distributors, and customers have no "fall-back position." Therefore, JIT logistics requires all participants to maintain quality and eliminate errors--to do the job right the first time. It also means knowing exactly what customers need and require in terms of stocks and service. Overall, JIT demands that all participating parties integrate plans and operations through shared information. Otherwise, when customers eliminate excess buffer inventory, they simply push it back onto their suppliers.

Any company in the supply-production-distribution-customer chain can tailor its operations to meet the explicit service requirements of its customers. To do so, the firm must determine how to deliver materials, products, or services so as to satisfy these requirements effectively and economically. The company can then determine what service levels it requires from its suppliers.

JIT logistics means establishing a long-term partnership with customers and suppliers, based on improved communications and procedures. It is an operating philosophy that encompasses a wide range of actions and changes focused on the following objectives:

- Creating vertical cooperation among all business partners

- Reducing inventories

- Increasing productivity

- Sharing technical expertise

- Improving product or service quality

- Reducing space needs

- Improving business communications with partners

Companies achieve these objectives by eliminating waste and properly involving personnel. Executives who were successful in these areas emphasized that you must recognize the importance of getting the right people in place to make JIT logistics work. Such a project takes careful planning, time, and effort, and requires sustained commitment by company managers. It must tie in with the overall strategy because of its far-reaching implications and requirements.

The benefits of this approach have proved so compelling that a leading consumer-goods manufacturer structures strategic alliances with all primary suppliers as an integral part of its new venture development process. The joint planning encompasses selecting technologies that simplify the combined manufacturing and distribution operations. In some cases, **each** partner makes financial investments to advance the overall opportunity that **none** would have made in a more traditional business arrangement.

ALLIANCES WITH CARRIERS AND WAREHOUSERS

Strategic alliances are by no means limited to vendors and customers. We found several companies asking carriers to provide sophisticated transportation services. These included:

- Dedication of drivers and equipment.
- Commitment to rigid pickup and delivery schedules and transit time standards.
- Implementation of new communications technology for reporting vehicle location and shipment status.
- Joint operations planning based on production and delivery schedules.

In structuring such alliances these firms are especially concerned with reducing or eliminating costly storage of inventory. They are evolving to the point where the only inventory they have consists of those materials in the transportation pipeline. This means that carriers must provide tightly coordinated, reliable transportation services.

One example of these alliances with carriers is American President Lines' parts-supply arrangement with New United Motor Manufacturing in Fremont, California. The plant, a joint venture between Toyota Motor Corporation and General Motors, sends a container chassis every morning to the steamship line's Oakland terminal to pick up a containerload of parts. Those parts, ordered five weeks previously, move directly from the container to the assembly line on the day they arrive.[9] In a similar arrangement, APL, working with a major railroad, delivers parts to a Toshiba assembly plant in Lebanon, Tennessee, via stack train each Monday--just in time for the week's scheduled production of microwave ovens and color televisions.

These transportation service arrangements often mean a carrier provides a "milk-run" service with daily pickups at multiple suppliers for delivery to the plant. Transportation, then, becomes an integral weapon in the war against inventory.

Another prime example of strategic alliances with carriers is the Federal Express PartsBank, a service operated by the well-known express delivery firm. PartsBank is specially designed to meet the field-support needs of the high-tech electronics/computer industries. Federal Express maintains a centralized parts warehouse for these customers. The carrier tailored its computer systems to maintain customer inventories and process immediate shipments. As a result, it can expedite critical items to any consumption point at any time, day or night. (Any part in the warehouse can be loaded on board one of the company's aircraft within 15 minutes.) Delivery turnaround time for these items averages about six hours. Instead of carrying redundant inventory at multiple regional warehouses, PartsBank customers can centralize all emergency parts in one warehouse and obtain 99 percent delivery reliability!

PartsBank customers report high standards of performance and true logistics cost savings in time-sensitive inventories. They also praise Federal Express's computer information, saying that orders, invoices, shipment tracking, and inventory controls are timely, accurate, and comprehensive.

We noted other strategic alliances that involved unique roles for public-warehouse companies. One company supports a major automotive plant by receiving shipments from several suppliers, combining related items, and preparing them for direct delivery to assembly points. Close coordination between suppliers, the warehouser, and the auto manufacturer has markedly reduced inventories throughout the supply chain.

Despite apparent benefits and strong interest in JIT logistics and other examples of strategic alliances, the learning process for U.S. companies is slow. American business is accustomed to buying innovations in the form of new tools and equipment. In contrast, strategic alliances require management to reshape corporate culture and create new attitudes toward planning, cooperation, and coordination.

Executives often ask how their companies can get started in developing strategic alliances for logistics. We offer the following advice. As a first step, management needs to understand the concept of value chains. It must review its major inbound and outbound channels and the respective roles played by each party (within and outside the company). In this process the value and costs added by each party should be challenged and alternatives should be considered and discussed with potential partners. This candid process of evaluation, challenge, and discussion was regarded by many executives we interviewed as the heart of structuring effective strategic alliances. This process results in an action plan for phasing an alliance into operations. A solid action plan is an essential ingredient because it determines the probability of success. Too often, business managers neglect to plan adequately for the focus, timing, communications, and adjustments necessary to implement logistics alliances.

Second, management should develop a program for changing the corporate culture such that quality and conformance to requirements become a way of life. In adopting this approach, one consumer-goods manufacturer trained over eight hundred workers, supervisors, and managers in the new methods they were adopting. Few companies are very flexible, so even with this intensive training, this culture change will take time. Several companies we interviewed stress that an environment of teamwork must be established in order to counter confusion and inefficiency. People in various departments have to work together as never before. The focus becomes the business as a whole rather than their own department or cost center.

Finally, strategic alliances cannot be put in place and then forgotten. Implementing an alliance requires an ongoing commitment to common strategic goals and objectives that can only be sustained through constant vigilance and adjustment.

Although many U.S. firms are dabbling with strategic alliances, few companies have installed programs that improve their supply and delivery operations to the point of creating competitive advantage. Obviously, operating with lower inventories helps reduce costs. The real advantage of these alliances, however, derives from the way in which they focus on the customer requirements that everyone in the chain is committed to meeting. A number of studies have shown that excellent customer service can increase market share. This fact places a new value on strategic alliances as a way to generate tangible competitive advantage.

Planning and executing effective alliances is not simple. It requires careful thought, coordination with customers and suppliers, and the support and education of all personnel. It also may require expenditures to prepare and sustain the operational changes. And it certainly requires the commitment of the senior-management team.

The payoffs, however, can be significant. Some companies are realizing cost savings from process improvements, and market-share growth from becoming preferred suppliers to their customers. The most successful company we encountered said its strategic alliances helped it achieve market-share growth of eight points--clearly an attractive achievement.

THE FUTURE OF STRATEGIC ALLIANCES

Like other principles of logistics excellence, formation of strategic alliances offers virtually unlimited opportunities for profit. Leading transportation companies are demonstrating how they can be full partners with manufacturers and merchandisers in the logistics chain. Similarly, innovative public-warehouse companies are formulating strong alliances, providing third-party storage and handling services.

As U.S. industry faces increasingly complex and competitive markets, logistics will play a larger role in serving customers. Those firms that best cultivate their strategic alliances with selected suppliers, carriers, distributors, and customers will achieve profit contributions beyond those that operate business as usual.

If this report is updated five to ten years from now, we are certain that creative strategic alliances will be prevalent in all industries. Entirely new kinds of win-win partnerships will emerge. We are confident that the profit potential for these alliances will exceed all current expectations.

Chapter 8

FOCUSING ON FINANCIAL PERFORMANCE

In recent writings, several prominent business authors suggested that perhaps the greatest problem faced today by established U.S. corporations is their bigness. The bigger the company, the easier it is for employees to pursue tangents and forget why the firm is in business in the first place--to increase the value of shareholders' investments.

We have seen many examples of this misdirection occurring in departments or divisions of organizations. Sales and marketing people worry about price competitiveness, so offer too many "loss leaders." Production managers focus on manufacturing costs at the expense of product quality. Purchasing agents become overly concerned about packaging costs, and overlook opportunities for creative packaging. And, logistics people worry so much about "cost-per-unit-handled" or other such measures that they lose sight of service quality.

A second problem of nearly as great importance is the focus on short-term results fostered by the investment industry's preoccupation with quarterly and annual results. Achieving and sustaining logistics excellence require vision and long-term commitment. Periodic financial performance should measure progress toward strategic goals and should not be an end in itself.

In our earlier books on transportation and warehousing, we devoted substantial space to the subject of identifying, measuring, accounting for, and reporting costs and investments.[10] We suggested means of monitoring performance and of identifying operating improvement opportunities. Happily, our research for this report revealed that many companies continue to improve the way they measure and analyze financial performance for logistics activities. This trend mirrors the more general business trend of companies' using return-on-assets (ROA) measures as their yardstick for profitability.

Indeed, by calculating return on logistics assets (ROLA) for facilities and equipment, firms get a clearer picture of profit contribution than by monitoring absolute cost levels. The most innovative firms we interviewed extend measurement of ROLA to their logistics partners, i.e., key vendors, distributors, and customers. They structure their strategic alliances based on careful analyses of revenues, costs, and investments throughout their major inbound and outbound channels. This results in each channel member's earning a return commensurate with its investment and the value it adds to the finished products. As a result, each channel member receives an adequate return **and** the price to consumers still provides attractive value.

The logistics sector in general, however, has a long way to go in this regard. The diversity in logistics financial management among companies remains great even within single industries. In our research, we encountered several "pairs of companies" that demonstrate the important implications of how we measure logistics financial performance. Typically, the two competitors sell identical products in identical markets. One firm monitors its costs "to death" while the other manages its logistics (and other) financial performance based on key success factors that measure not only asset utilization and productivity factors but also **customer value** added by logistics. Invariably, the former wonders why its market share is not higher, even though its profits are adequate for the time being as a result of stringent cost control.

Our intent in this chapter is not to transform readers into financial managers or analysts. Nor is it to delve into specific techniques of financial analysis. Other books and seminars do both jobs more than adequately. Instead, we hope to persuade executives to challenge the way in which the financial performance of their firm's **business operations** is measured--with logistics being the focus here. Such challenges should concentrate broadly on strategic objectives and on performance in meeting them, not narrowly on cost accounting, physical units of measure, or transportation/warehousing expenses. **Quantifying** performance **is** important but as we describe below, the measures we use must go beyond physical resources consumed and costs incurred. Moreover, any review should be oriented toward consistent measures over time, not short-term parameters such as this month's results. Is this reorientation difficult? No, it shouldn't be. If we return to the basics, and determine how logistics helps the business make a profit, we can then decide how to measure its performance.

FINANCIAL MANAGEMENT AND LOGISTICS

Top management's recent preoccupation with corporate-wide cost reductions has heightened the focus within logistics departments on financial management. This focus was slow in coming. It began emerging only after the industry was "beaten over the head" with the idea. Leading business authors like Peter Drucker pinpointed logistics as an "untapped jungle." A major productivity study sponsored by the Council of Logistics Management in 1978 called logistics a "$40-billion gold mine." And transportation deregulation forced managers to see that millions of dollars were being spent--often unnecessarily--to move products.

This new financial focus is appropriate. Measuring the cost of logistics to the company has been a useful exercise. In some cases, top management saw, for the first time, the total costs of logistics, and couldn't believe the numbers. The reports were sent back for further analysis! They were shocked to learn that logistics costs could represent up to 40 percent of the cost of sales.

The continuing quest for logistics productivity, stemming largely from the heightened cost consciousness, also has value. Shorter customer-service cycles, reduced inventories, and greater equipment utilization are worthy goals. And, as we stated in our previous reports, more timely, reliable, and comprehensive information on costs and investments improves company operations.

This focus on logistics financial management has evolved to the point where several major companies appointed managers with financial backgrounds to head up their logistics operations. Notable among these firms are Gillette, Thomas J. Lipton, and Baxter Travenol Laboratories. In these cases, logistics performance has improved as a direct result of the new financial orientation.

In our previous two reports, we recommended that a finance manager and staff be incorporated into the logistics organization to actively oversee the department's cost-management efforts. Many companies have taken this step. At Baxter Travenol Laboratories, for example, the finance manager reports to the director of operations and materials management who, in turn, reports to the vice-president of logistics. Baxter Travenol's logistics finance organization encompasses financial operations (the department controller), freight payments, and data control.

This kind of organization makes sense at Baxter Travenol, because the company operates on the premise that ownership of the budget should fall to the operations director responsible for delivering results in that area. The director sets targets for the function (such as cost per case), and the finance manager sees that results are measured and reported properly. Of course, the logistics financial manager coordinates all activities with corporate finance and accounting to maintain a consistent framework and process for cost management.

In our previous reports, we also recommended that logistics executives stop relying solely on corporate financial organizations for financial management, and learn these skills themselves. This recommendation stemmed from the fact that many logistics managers rise through the ranks in operating positions, and do not receive adequate training in the financial effects of their decisions. Sadly, this situation still exists in many companies.

While logistics executives may recognize such shortcomings in themselves and their staffs, too often their solutions are inadequate. As we mentioned above, one solution relies on bringing a financial manager into the logistics "fold" to "worry about costs," "create the budget," and the like. This approach may produce some benefits, but it has several shortcomings:

- It doesn't improve or require understanding of financial consequences by all logistics managers.

- It encourages reactive rather than proactive behavior.

- It doesn't foster department-wide commitment to critical financial and other quantitative goals.

- It reduces logistics managers' ability to quantify logistics' effects on decisions involving manufacturing and sales.

Unresolved, these problems hamper profitability. Consider an important effect of the Tax Reform Act of 1986. This legislation impacted distributors because it contained a provision that creates "uniform capitalization" rules for inventories. These rules require that virtually all costs related to purchasing, repackaging, and warehousing goods must be capitalized in inventory. As a result, the Act increased the taxable income of distributors, and complicated recordkeeping. The logistics financial manager working alone probably spotted this problem. But did the firm's distribution executives share the responsibility for addressing the business issues adequately and making the right company-wide decisions as to costs, prices, and procedures? Probably not.

Another way logistics managers try to fill their lack of financial-management expertise is by relying excessively on volumes of computer-generated data. With expanded use of personal computers in business, many logistics people become "instant experts" in financial management. Software programs enable them to track budgets, expenses, and cost indicators easily. Thus, they believe the "problem is solved." On the contrary--they have more information at their disposal, but it is **activity-related**, not **results-related**, so it does not improve the quality of strategic decision making.

As an example, logistics managers at a large grocery-products manufacturer believed the installation of new software packages would provide them sufficient information to manage their function. Indeed, the systems did generate better information on activities, so the managers had a clearer idea of activity costs. But the systems did not help management forecast or simulate costs or assess the overall impact of logistics on revenues. Thus, they had little strategic impact on the distribution executives' ability to manage the function's financial performance.

In addition, the inability of the company's logistics managers to use sound financial management tools relegated logistics to a weak secondary role in the planning of promotions and new products--both of which are key to the success of food processors in today's marketplace. As a result, corporate planning, sales, and marketing people assumed average values for the logistics costs associated with promotions and new products...values which turned out to be inaccurate. Pricing decisions were based on inaccuracies, and new products were distributed without adequate planning for the logistics cost impacts. Had the logistics managers been effective financial managers, these mistakes would not have been made.

As we emphasized in Chapter 3, linking logistics strategy to corporate strategy is one key to logistics excellence. Proper financial management of logistics functions is critical to that process. Knowing the financial consequences of logistics activities is essential to forward planning. And managing operations based on their **broad** financial effects is necessary for achieving performance that is consistent with strategic objectives and plans.

The problems of one consumer-goods manufacturer illustrate this latter point. The loss of an important customer prompted an "investigation" to find the cause. Initially, the problem was attributed to logistics--chronically poor fill rates. Further analysis showed that new logistics inventory reduction steps coincided with a drop in manufacturing yields (due to cheaper ingredients) and introduction of new promotions that marketing had not properly communicated to production planning and inventory management. Each department was pursuing strategic objectives of reduced cost or increased sales, yet their lack of coordination proved to be a financial catastrophe that took months to correct.

TRADITION VS. RELEVANCE

Financial-management expertise has not been a priority of logistics managers because of the way in which the function's performance traditionally was measured. Specifically, we refer to the practice of measuring **costs** such as freight, labor, and warehouse rates. Because these costs are readily attributed to the logistics manager, the company adopts them as measures of logistics financial performance.

This narrow focus ignores the most important factors influencing costs of logistics, which relate directly to the nature of the overall business strategy. We illustrate this point in the chart below.

106

	Logistics Controllable	Other Controllable
● Labor Costs		
Pay Scales		X
Fringe Benefits		X
Activity Level		X
Productivity	X	
● Transportation Costs		
Product Characteristics		X
Customer Service Requirements		X
Customer Size		X
Customer Location		X
Freight Rates	X	
● Warehousing Costs		
Product Characteristics		X
Forecast Accuracy		X
Customer Service Requirements		X
Seasonality		X
Warehouse Rates	X	

Note that those costs listed as "other controllable" have a greater impact on overall logistics performance than the three narrow factors in the logistics controllable column. The latter determine something less than 20 percent of total logistics costs. We recognize that the typical logistics organization controls few variables in the overall cost equation. Many of the variables are influenced primarily by factors controlled by senior management such as how we choose to organize, manage, and compensate. Nevertheless, logistics managers can and should supply performance input that influences all of them.

Most logistics and financial executives don't take the time to understand which variables are independent and which are controllable. Even when they do, they fail to realize that certain performance criteria, such as those dictating customer-service policies and practices, may exist because of corporate inertia. Many companies, for instance, perpetuate ineffective order entry, processing, and invoicing procedures because of constraints set by outdated computer systems. Rather than making incremental changes in their systems to effect small, but tangible, improvements, logistics and sales managers blame the system for problems, but say they are powerless to make changes.

Measurement of key logistics success factors that relate to strategic business plans can positively affect corporate profitability. Fortunately, more logistics and financial managers are getting comfortable with the concept of "total logistics-system costs," i.e., product cost from raw material to customer delivery. Also, some companies, as described below, have developed effective approaches for determining the factors that are critical to achieving their logistics strategic objectives. Why then do we not see more logistics financial-performance reports on total costs and value, or on customer-service measures that directly influence sales levels and profitability? Tradition, departmental "walls," and resistance to change stand in the way.

Yet, success stories, such as the total logistics-system cost approach in place at Xerox Corporation, illustrate the value of change. The logistics executives at Xerox's Business Systems Group transformed a typical logistics "cost center" into a department that emulates the behavior of a profit center to better meet its strategic objectives. The Business Systems Group employs some 1,200 people in the logistics/distribution area, and manages over $250 million in parts and consumable inventories throughout the logistics pipeline. To change its focus, the logistics department follows four key steps:

Establish benchmarks. Available industry data is used to create benchmarks for expenses, inventory turns, and service levels. Then, a "market value" is established for functions performed by logistics.

Negotiate service levels. The department sets up a "fee schedule" based on expenses and service degrees, and negotiated level-of-service contracts with its internal customers (other Xerox units).

Bid for business. The department solicits business from other Xerox divisions, bidding against competing logistics units or outside service contractors. In this way, the company obtains good service at competitive rates.

Sell to outsiders. The logistics department can (and does) contract to provide the full complement of distribution services to non-Xerox companies. Or, it can supply individual distribution services such as warehousing for these outside clients.

The benefits to Xerox of this "profit-center" approach far exceed simple efficiency improvements in the company's logistics operations. The system forces other divisions (customers) to define their true service needs, recognizing the costs involved. As a result, they purchase only the level of service they need, and no more. That, in turn, allows logistics managers to structure their operations to provide the scope and levels of service truly needed to support the overall business plan. As a result, the company has recorded unprecedented logistics productivity improvements averaging 12 percent for the last three years. At the same time, service satisfaction has become evident among customers and the other Xerox business units they support.

TOMORROW'S FOCUS: FINANCIAL AND ECONOMIC PERFORMANCE MEASURES

At financially oriented companies like Xerox, logistics departments are changing the way they evaluate operating performance from a focus on short-term profit to one of longer-term return on assets (ROA). They find the ROA measure more meaningful even than return on sales, primarily because the former measures "how we are doing" in terms of managing our logistics assets investments. These assets include traditional items such as inventories, warehousing facilities/equipment, and private fleets, and more recently, computer hardware and software.

Increasing emphasis on ROA has prompted many companies to "redeploy" (sometimes meaning eliminate) certain assets. For example, hundreds of companies have redeployed cash invested in private truck fleet assets. Under deregulation, shippers gained access to more creative carrier service/price options. Thus, numerous firms reduced or eliminated their private fleets in favor of establishing partnerships with strong carriers.

As a measure of performance, ROA is a clear improvement over pure cost-focused measures. We believe, however, that, in the current U.S. business environment, measuring financial performance will require new and creative approaches. These must be geared toward measuring economic value added (not merely accounting costs) and linked to business strategy. This thought is based on the belief expressed by many we interviewed that the best measure of a company's operating performance is the rate-of-return on total capital relative to the company's weighted average cost of capital, or "hurdle rate." This attitude has become a basic tenet of investment analysis. Management must expect to do as well with the funds it invests in the company as investors could do for themselves by investing the money elsewhere. Thus, the cost of capital is not a cash cost, but rather an "opportunity cost."

What does this point have to do with logistics performance? A lot, we believe. First, astute investors evaluate companies based on economic and financial criteria related closely to strategic issues, not solely on accounting cost measures. Thus, operating performance is measured in terms of how the business is doing in managing the assets associated with main activities of the enterprise. Investors focus on broader financial measures of operating performance, including asset turnover and operating margins with ROA. In addition, they will increasingly compare a company to the competing firms in its key markets. These comparisons often provide significant insight into how successful the company will be in achieving its strategic financial objectives.

Second, the increasing emphasis on value-added services will require closer measures of the type and quantity of value being added to the firm's products by its logistics activities. As a vice-president of logistics stated, "At our company, if a person cannot demonstrate he/she is adding value to a product, we take appropriate action (to remedy the situation)." A department that simply stores, handles, or transports materials or products is inadequate in today's highly competitive markets. We must demonstrate that our logistics strategies and activities add value and create competitive advantage.

This increasing awareness of value-added logistics services is leading us to measure the function in such terms as "economic value added." For logistics operations, economic value added might mean the dollar measure of all logistics operations or services. As an example, for the Xerox logistics operations we described above, management could evaluate logistics-department performance by using the following equation:

Logistics Economic Value Added = Total beginning logistics investment times (the return on logistics investment minus the return that could be achieved elsewhere).

While this calculation requires the company to find a way to measure returns, the fact that Xerox's logistics-services customers are specifying the services they require, and paying for them, means that expected performance levels must be achieved. In this case, logistics performance--in terms of value added--becomes the return on capital invested (amount spent on logistics services). Investments of comparable risk would consist of alternative outside services, such as other carriers, public warehouses, and the like.

The logistics economic value added of the logistics department relates to its "market value," or value the department has in its marketplace. We can even factor into the analysis a premium (or discount) for the "quality of logistics management," similar to the approach to valuing industry-specific companies (e.g., steel, computers, etc.) in investment-banking circles.

Measuring logistics performance in economic and financial terms that are broader than total cost levels offers significant benefits to the business with respect to logistics and other operations. First, it demands that we link performance with strategy. Defining value-added logistics services demands that we specify what the business unit (or company) plans to achieve, and then line up the services against these objectives. In short, we allocate resources to attain specific, quantifiable business goals.

The second benefit accrues from thinking of logistics as a profit-contributor, rather than just a cost center. Certainly, the customer pays a "price" for logistics services, just as in traditional situations the company provided logistics services at a cost. When logistics performance is measured in terms of value-added return, however, we must identify, measure, and demonstrate what value warehousing, transportation, inventories, and the like add to the firm's products. We develop this concept further in Chapter 9, "Targeting Optimum Service Levels."

The third plus associated with monitoring logistics by more comprehensive financial and economic measures lies in the fact that this approach demands that management do a better job of financial planning with logistics-department and business-unit customers. The relationship between a unit's operating and financial strategies is based on the sources and uses of funds. Operating cash flow--or cash operating profit minus financing --can be the link between the business plan and the financing plan.

Thus, the logistics department must plan as an operating profit center would, i.e., achieve net operating revenues at least equal to net operating expenses. This requires that management identify, measure, and forecast operating costs under various business scenarios, and price services accordingly. For the business unit or customer, this approach necessitates a type of financial planning that anticipates **returns** from logistics expenses.

This means that if the manufacturing or marketing unit adopts the principle that quality logistics returns value to the firm, and that sales will increase through improved customer service, then logistics management is in the position to specify what financial returns it expects. In this scenario, logistics "buyers" also gain sophistication as to what values can be bought, measured, and achieved.

Finally, measuring logistics performance through ROA and other financial measures permits us to evaluate **each** service provided as a stand-alone value. Therefore, we can assess by product group, location, customer, channel, or other parameters exactly how much value is created by the logistics services contracted for. By comparing financial performance of the service--costs and revenues generated--against the buyer's cost of capital, we can evaluate whether the logistics investment was warranted.

PERSPECTIVE ON LOGISTICS FINANCIAL PERFORMANCE

The measurement concepts suggested above are somewhat new to logistics executives. They are not new, however, to business leaders and financial executives. As logistics-performance measurement begins to mirror business-performance measurement, management will gain a broader understanding of the value associated with logistics.

Examples of companies that have converted logistics operations to profit centers exist in several industries. Most involve restructuring the firm's use of its private fleet not only to meet the service needs of the corporation, but to turn a profit. Adding "logistics" as a major new product line should **not** be the company's emphasis. Logistics and financial executives need to progress beyond these examples to fully achieve business value. The Xerox case of profit-center emulation represents the forefront of an emerging trend toward a business philosophy of operations. The Xerox approach focuses on identifying the **real** logistics service needs of internal and external customers, i.e., those requirements that someone is willing to pay to have met. Other companies certainly will follow Xerox's lead.

Logistics executives may note that we have written an entire cost-oriented chapter without referring to logistics "trade-offs." Certainly, we do not dismiss the basic fact that the component activities of physical distribution (transportation, warehousing, inventory, service, information, etc.) have associated costs that must be "traded-off" against one another to achieve an "optimum" distribution operation. Indeed, our research showed that until recently many logistics decisions heavily focused on minimizing total logistics costs. We found, however, numerous companies that took a broader view of logistics decisions, which requires that scarce resources be allocated to physical distribution (place), as well as to product, price, and promotion (the marketing mix). The objective here is to allocate resources to all "four Ps" of the marketing mix in a manner that will generate the greatest long-term profits.

In lieu of emphasizing trade-off issues, we chose to concentrate on gauging the financial performance of logistics functions in terms most relevant to the business strategy of the company. If this strategy positions the firm as the low-cost producer/supplier of a group of products, then minimizing logistics costs as measured by total-cost analysis is consistent, and financial performance should be evaluated in that manner.

As we stress throughout this book, however, logistics can (and does) influence profitability in more ways than costs. Therefore, its financial performance should be measured in terms of what value it adds to the products it supports. We know of only a few large corporations that maintain the simple low-cost producer strategy. Most recognize the business value of pursuing competitive advantage, through product or service differentiation. Consequently, we need to create new ways of measuring logistics' financial performance that reflect these types of strategies.

American industry as a whole faces sluggish growth for the balance of this decade. Thus, cost savings will continue to be a major part of most business strategies, especially in overhead accounts where value-added functions are less tangible. However, the innovative practices and guidelines described above support this strategy equally well. By measuring the financial performance of logistics functions in terms such as economic value added, we require logistics to produce value in return for the company's investment in its people, facilities, equipment, and information systems.

Chapter 9

TARGETING OPTIMUM SERVICE LEVELS

Although customers and companies define the term customer service somewhat differently, most agree that good service comes down to three basic elements: availability, convenience, and information. This means the buyer expects to get the right product, at the right place, at the right time, in good condition. He/she expects to expend a minimum amount of administrative effort to get the goods and pay for them. And, the customer expects to be advised promptly if the supplier is unable, or expects to be unable, to deliver the complete order on time.

These expectations may sound simple and straightforward, but making them a reality is another matter. We found numerous companies that have made customer-service improvement one of their strategic objectives, but several expressed frustration at not achieving their goals. We find that their experience is not unique. The sad truth is that most American companies--despite the fact that they acknowledge customers as essential to their business--pay too little attention to guaranteeing effective customer service. Precious few companies serve their customers well all the time.

Why do businesses fail their customers in the service area? Based on our research and dealings with hundreds of clients and their customers, we believe there are three reasons for service breakdowns:

- Company managers don't know enough about what their customers **really** want.

- The company's customer-service strategy is either non-existent, too general, or **not linked directly to daily operations**.

- The sheer size of the customer base (often in the thousands) necessitates the involvement of many corporate departments and personnel. Inconsistency results.

Quality customer service can create competitive advantage. More and more U.S. firms are realizing this fact. Nevertheless, relatively few companies, we find, have taken the necessary steps to achieve this. Specifying a customer-service strategy as part of the overall logistics and business strategies is a critical beginning. Making "satisfaction of customer requirements" a part of the corporate culture (not just an afterthought) is an important corollary. Such basic actions have contributed to the success of several leading companies. In this chapter, we address these issues and discuss how companies can establish the kind of effective customer service that creates competitive advantage.

WHAT IS CUSTOMER SERVICE IN LOGISTICS?

Logistics customer service has many definitions and applications. At E.I. du Pont, for example, customer service comprises the organization that operates field warehouses and handles such finished-goods functions as order entry and processing. This department is charged with implementing E.I. du Pont's corporate policy of quality service to customers. Unlike many other companies, however, Du Pont sees customer service as more than a department to process and ship individual orders. For several months, E.I. du Pont has been studying the unique customer-service needs of its customers and markets and evaluating how best to structure its operations to meet those needs. The goal is to invest in the **right** kinds and levels of service--no more and no less.

At many other companies, however, no such organization or focus exists. Gould's Industrial Automation Division at one time maintained a customer-service organization as a separate profit center for post-delivery support (service and repair) of the company's factory-automation products. (This kind of set-up, which emphasizes service only as it relates to repair support, is common among "high-tech" industries.) In fact, Gould's repair service assumed such pre-eminence that it threatened to overpower the company's new-product distribution. The division developed problems with order entry and processing, product delivery, and other aspects of finished-goods management. By re-thinking the meaning of customer service, Gould management adjusted its operations to reflect a better balance between product support and new-product distribution.

The grocery-products industry places a high value on customer service. Product must be available in time to be delivered when needed, with rapid turnover at wholesale and retail levels. The interactions this requires between logistics, production, and sales must work smoothly to achieve these service levels. Companies vary in how they organize to achieve these goals. At Ralston Purina Co., the customer-service manager is based at the finished-goods warehouse at each plant and works directly with the plant manager. He/she has the authority to coordinate production, inventory, and transportation operations in order to focus plant activities on customer needs. The customer order backlog and specific customer and market requirements (managed centrally by the logistics department) drive the customer-service manager's actions. This broad view of customer service helps Ralston Purina be more responsive in meeting customer requirements and is, they feel, a key factor in profitability.

While several views of customer service exist, we define it in very simple terms. Effective customer service means creating in your customers' minds the perception that your organization is "easy to do business with." It means your company is sensitive to customers' needs, and finds creative and innovative ways to address them effectively. Unfortunately, people, corporate cultures, and a number of other factors tend to complicate these simple goals.

The customer-service mission is not easy. A quick look at six basic elements of customer service illustrates its potential for complexity. These elements include:

- **Product availability**--the capability to supply the items and quantities on an order on the first shipment.

- **Order cycle time**--the time elapsed between customer order submission and receipt of goods.

- **Distribution information**--the ability to provide accurate and timely information on inventory status, order acknowledgment and status, invoicing, etc.

- **Distribution flexibility**--the ability to respond to special needs and situations, e.g., to expedite special requests, product substitutions, or modifications, etc.

- **Post-delivery support**--being able to meet post-delivery customer needs, e.g., handling returned goods, providing technical advice and repairs, etc.

- **Order-servicing quality**--performing all activities necessary to correctly fill, invoice, and collect for an order, based on the customer requirements.

Obviously, a lot can go wrong within each of these elements, particularly in companies with high volumes of orders, stockkeeping units, and customers. In fact, we can almost match up these elements with "typical" customer complaints, identified and ranked in most surveys or studies as the following:

- Late deliveries

- Product or quality mistakes

- Damaged goods

- Frequent shortages

- Others (inaccurate or ill-timed information, for example)

Furthermore, these same studies identify five common customer reactions to service failures. The clients:

- Reduced their volume of purchases with the problem supplier or discontinued the whole line

- Refused to purchase new items

- Refused to support promotions

- Called in the salesman or manager to air complaints

- Took billing adjustments or delayed payment to "compensate" for customer-service problems

Because the consequences of poor customer service can be so dire, we believe every company should view customer service as critical to profitability and success.

THE SUPPLY CHAIN VS. DEMAND MANAGEMENT

Earlier in this report, we briefly discussed the role of the value chain in determining corporate strategy and competitive advantage. We also talked (in Chapter 5) about "demand management," and how this philosophy can enhance the value of the company's information systems. In addressing customer service, we think it important to re-visit these concepts to understand how the best companies target customer-service strategies for profit.

One of the business philosophies currently emerging in industry is "supply-chain management." This concept stems from the realization that firms operate within a pipeline or chain that extends from raw-materials suppliers to finished-goods customers--"from the grain field to the pantry," so to speak. The philosophy helps companies understand their role in getting products to customers. It also helps managers create strategic alliances, channel systems, and other partnerships that "add value" to their products beyond their efficient physical movement.

The supply-chain management philosophy has one major flaw, however. It envisions a business world in which products are supplied or "pushed" to customers. Overzealous application of this concept, therefore, contradicts the basic reason companies are in business--i.e., to produce products that customers want and need. Strict interpretation of supply-chain management disregards the fundamental business premise that products should be "pulled" through the channel in tune to customer needs.

We have visited companies at which managers prided themselves on approaching their business with a value-added, supply-chain perspective. When we analyzed their customer-service strategy and operations, however, we often found activities directed by an underlying "push" attitude that gave incentives to the sales force, distributors, or retailers for "getting rid of the product."

Too often, this attitude does not change until the business sustains a tangible penalty that is clearly linked to customer-service performance. Consumer-products firms that compete aggressively for shelf space, for example, know all too well that the penalty for poor customer service is lost shelf position and lost sales. Industrial-products companies, and other industries, have their own "battlefields." Often, alarming sales declines and resulting inventory build-ups preview the resulting decline in profits that can result from poor customer service.

In contrast to the supply-chain approach, the "demand-management" philosophy can help prevent such penalty actions. The focus here is on encouraging the customer to buy our products. Thinking in terms of how to meet **demand** for one's products, not just how to **supply** them, can help managers focus on meeting customer needs. The old adage that manufacturing creates product quality, sales and marketing generate product attraction, and physical distribution provides service is no longer adequate. Rather, all managers--regardless of their department--must concern themselves with creating and filling demand. Product quality is essential; but without good customer service, not even quality can produce sales and profit. A lot of warehouses are filled with quality products that collect dust because their producers lack effective distribution-service structures. Recently, a number of microcomputer firms demonstrated this phenomenon. Cutting-edge technology and top quality proved inadequate to overcome distribution-service shortcomings.

ESTABLISHING CUSTOMER-SERVICE STRATEGY

The best customer-service organizations recognize there is an economic trade-off between the cost of providing improved service and the incremental profits generated from resulting increased sales. Below, we suggest an "optimum" approach to analyzing these trade-offs, based on financial criteria. This optimization model defines all the economic variables inherent in the cost-benefit analysis. The trade-off analysis depicted in the exhibit below is based on the ability to identify and quantify incremental revenue resulting from changes in customer-service levels.[11]

Optimal Distribution Service Level
Maximum Contribution to Profit

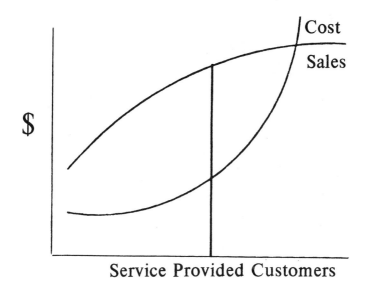

Service Provided Customers

In reality, however, factors like changes in competitors' service levels, stress on the marketplace, capacity restraints, etc., make practical application of such a model difficult. So we can better justify our service costs by taking a common-sense approach and, perhaps, assessing whether the expense-to-sales ratio is consistent with our strategic objectives.

The best companies follow several basic steps in developing a good customer-service strategy. As a general rule, they make it a point to "know how they're doing" at all times. Through service performance measurements, customer discussions, meetings with sales and other field units, and the like, these firms know whether their customer-service programs are working.

In creating a customer-service strategy, these firms first establish or update their current policy by going directly to customers to establish their real needs and how well the company and its competitors are meeting them.

They set up a concise, market-oriented program that identifies where the firm is going. The program quantitatively articulates how the unit plans to serve its customers with respect to basic inventory types. For example:

Inventory Class	Desired Percent Sales	Service Level	Order Cycle Time
A	60%	95%-98%	2 Days
B	20%	90%-95%	5 Days
C	15%	90%-95%	10 Days
D	3%	85%-90%	20 Days
E	2%		Based on manufacturing lead time

Note: The service policy differs by inventory group, and the service parameters for each stock category are based on extensive analysis of customer needs and competitive environment. It serves as the foundation for determining the needed levels and uses of the physical, financial, systems, and human resources.

Step 2 requires designing or reconfiguring the distribution-center network. The firm needs to locate product in a manner that efficiently meets order-cycle commitments, while minimizing warehousing, transportation, inventory-carrying and customer-service costs.

As the next step, the company should make sure its human resources are effective. Each distribution center needs managers who know their business, operate as a team, and focus on serving customers. It is top management's job to see these people receive adequate, ongoing training, and to reward their successes.

Finally, we come to the "hard," but most important part of customer service. We refer to the targeting or setting of detailed service criteria for specific markets, individual customers, and/or particular product groups.

Service is expensive, but by finely targeting service levels, companies can reduce unnecessary expenditures.

This step often involves a great deal of insight and creativity. For example, one medical products company incorporated specific level of service commitments into its comprehensive contracts that focused on volume and pricing issues. This created a more attractive overall package and improved market share.

An electronics manufacturer recognized the need for higher service levels for products on promotion. By meeting its customers' service requirements for these items, the firm achieved sales and margin increases that more than made up for the required increase in distribution cost.

CUSTOMER SERVICE--CONTRIBUTION TO PROFIT

Distribution service and marketing success are inextricably linked. A distribution function that provides proper levels of service and satisfies customer needs can increase sales and market share, and ultimately can contribute to corporate profitability and growth. Conversely, when the distribution function is poorly executed and fails to satisfy customer requirements, sales and market share decline and distribution's contribution to profit drops.

We draw these conclusions from nearly ten years of study of distribution-service performance in many industries.[12] Our analyses were designed to identify the specific elements of distribution service that caused customers (the ultimate purchaser, or even the intermediate purchasing agent) to do more or less business with given suppliers.

Specifically, our research shows that:

- Suppliers can increase market share through superior service, applied selectively.

- The important components of distribution service can be identified and their impact on sales measured.

These facts are the foundation upon which leading companies build their service strategies. Providing superior service carries a cost, so management's challenge lies in finding the service/cost equation that provides the maximum difference between revenues achieved and costs incurred.

As we stated, the sales impact of customer service can be measured, as can the costs of providing this service. In addition, computerized mathematical evaluation can identify the specific service that generates a maximum contribution to profit. Thus, the "value" of service (as measured by customers' sales responses) can be established and used to improve overall profitability.

In the final analysis, distribution and the customer service it provides has one principal objective--to provide value to the customer, which ultimately contributes to company sales, market share, profitability, and growth. If physical distribution is viewed solely as a cost, management probably will do all it can to pare this expense to a minimum. A minimum-cost distribution program, however, usually can't deliver the service levels necessary to benefit sales and profits. Instead, this approach actually may create problems for the firm.

Given this fact, can optimal distribution-service levels be identified for every company? Can they be identified within each company for each market, region, customer group, product line, season, type of sales (promotional vs. regular), etc., in order to develop the best service policy and distribution systems design? The answer to these questions is yes.

In targeting optimum service levels, management needs to remember at all times that service should meet the basic needs of the buyer. Buyers evaluate suppliers' ability to satisfy their needs based on performance in the following areas:

- Total order-cycle time

- On-time delivery

- Delivery reliability and consistency

- Order completeness--lines, quantities

- Response to emergency requirements

- Service during promotions

- Response to customer inquiries and complaints

- Order accuracy

- Inventory in-stock service levels

- Condition of product on delivery

- "Presence in the market"

- Quantity price structure (minimum order size, quantity price breaks)

Clearly, some of these factors are more important than others.

For each element, therefore, it is critical to establish appropriate performance levels. Some will demand high levels resulting perhaps in high cost. Others will be less important, presenting opportunities for cost reductions. Finding the right combination, therefore, is critical to designing the optimal distribution service package.

Service-level needs vary according to industry, company, product, trade channel, customer type, season, economic environment, promotional versus regular sales, name-brand strength (market share), planned versus impulse purchasing, and profitability level. For example, some companies that dominate a market believe they can afford occasional service lapses. Other companies in a similar position firmly believe they can not. They feel such weaknesses open the door to competitors and result in ongoing costs of fighting competition that are often well in excess of the cost of meeting customers' service needs. This apparent dichotomy underscores the need to link the customer service strategy with the overall business philosophy of the organization.

The sales curve illustrated below shows what effect expanded distribution service can have on sales. Notice that as service increases, sales rise. The rate of sales increase slows down, however, as service nears 100 percent performance. This fact is important, because it indicates there is an identifiable, practical limit to the amount of increased service to be provided.

Optimal Distribution Service Level
Maximum Contribution to Profit

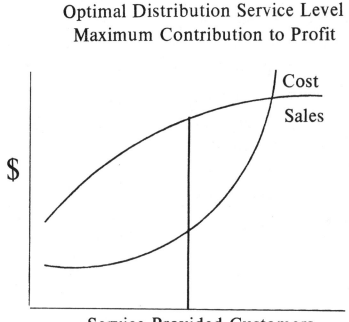

As service levels rise, the costs of providing service escalate rapidly, as the cost curve shows. At some point, the costs associated with capturing the additional sales outstrip their profit contribution.

A cursory study of these curves might lead one to assume that the intersection point of the two lines represents optimum service levels. Not true. The best distribution-service program balances service and cost to provide the **maximum difference** between revenues achieved and costs incurred. This point is represented by the vertical line in the chart. The line shows the place at which the two curves are the farthest apart, i.e., the point of maximum contribution to profit.

Achieving the right service balance can have direct and indirect effects on sales. The direct effect is apparent where service impacts market share and sales. The indirect effect shows up in buyer preference in supplier selection.

Chronic stock-outs or late shipments, for example, cause eventual shortages on the retail shelf or in the industrial stock pile. These stock-outs translate directly into lost sales. At the same time, these service failures have a longer-term impact. Buyers prefer to do business with suppliers that offer better service or cause fewer problems. In addition, these buyers are more likely to accept new products, provide more shelf space, accept proposed promotions, and be slower to drop an item currently carried for their reliable suppliers. Conversely, a buyer suffering from poor supplier service may take one of the penalty actions listed earlier--drop an item, refuse a new listing, refuse promotions, reduce shelf space, etc.

SUSTAINING EFFECTIVENESS IN CUSTOMER SERVICE

As we said above, the most effective customer service is that which provides consistent, tailored levels of performance. Naturally, distribution operations must be organized to enable the firm to achieve these levels. In many cases, a certain amount of logistics-network reshuffling may be necessary to implement a focused service program. Examples of such changes include:

- Altering the field-warehouse configuration to maximize sales potential, i.e., providing better service to major markets through increased product availability and increased "presence" in key major markets, and reducing unneeded expenditures in markets where present service represents overkill.

- Increasing inventory availability at selected stocking points, thereby improving order fill to meet new objectives. Better availability can increase sales, and reduce transportation demands by eliminating cross-territory shipping.

- Reducing the number of field points at which given items are stocked, thereby reducing investment in inventory.

- Shipping different sizes of orders from more economical sources for given markets; making more plant-direct shipments, thereby reducing field inventories.

- Merchandising the improved service levels as part of the marketing program.

- Scientifically monitoring and measuring the response of sales and costs to each element of the new distribution-service strategy. Each change implemented should serve two purposes: to increase profitability; and to improve information for future decision making.

This latter action enables the best companies to sustain effectiveness in their distribution and customer-service performance. By monitoring and measuring service properly, and by adjusting service as conditions change, firms can stay ahead. Otherwise, any competitive advantage derived from a particular action will diminish over time.

Most U.S. companies have worked hard to minimize the costs of distribution. For those who work harder at increasing its contribution to profit, and targeting their customer service, the payoffs in sales and market-share gains can be dramatic. The second group truly uses distribution service as a competitive weapon, and its relentless commitment to customer-service excellence pays off.

Chapter 10
MANAGING THE DETAILS

In doing the research for this project, we briefed a number of top logistics executives on what we considered the 10 principles of logistics excellence. One such individual took issue with our decision to include "managing the details" on the list. He argued that most managers don't have the time or resources to oversee the details of their logistics operation. In his case, he holds a corporate position in materials management and oversees logistics in 54 strategic business units in which 8,500 people work. "How could I possibly worry about the details?" he asked.

Later in our discussion, after we described the principle further, the executive agreed that detail-management really is essential. However, he helped us refine the principle to focus on managing the **right** details. In addition, he pointed out the crucial need for large firms to establish common methodologies for controlling important details, so as to ensure logistics' contribution to profit. Use of common techniques helps focus management's attention on the right areas on a consistent basis. We are often asked what is meant by details; which are important; and what are the right details on which to focus. A definitive answer is illusive and situational. The heart of the issue lies in a company's strategic objectives and in its detailed customer requirements. A detail is important if performing or managing it properly affects customer satisfaction or achievement of our strategic objectives.

For example, one business equipment manufacturer was particularly plagued by customer complaints involving various delivery, installation, and billing problems. The situation was becoming serious; sales were affected and repeat orders were more difficult to achieve. After studying exactly how they filled orders and the kinds of things that were causing the complaints, they launched a "no-fault" installation program. The program targeted over twenty logistics-related activities (i.e., "details") that were important to the customers' perception that they had received exactly what they ordered, when they needed it, and that they could use it when it arrived.

This company is not alone. Many others have learned the hard way that sound strategies, superior products, and creative marketing, while important, are not enough to ensure success. Careful attention to important implementation details are key to turning the other elements into profitable operations.

BACK TO BASICS IN LOGISTICS

Critics of American industry today say that excessive complexity, extensive strategic planning, and overemphasis on form versus substance seriously damage our global business position. The critics say a return to business basics is the way to regain the lost ground. Although somewhat simplistic, this view contains a kernel of truth.

If business in general suffers from over-strategizing, logistics exhibits similar symptoms. Too often, management excels at creating strategy and addressing broader issues such as cost/service trade-offs, but falls short in making day-to-day improvements. Management neglects to recognize or understand the "minor" problems and thereby creates greater problems.

Take, for example, sales and distribution departments that make every order an "exception." Their efforts to provide extra "sales flexibility" make it impossible for any software program to work properly. The resulting order-processing delays annoy customers to the point of creating **real** sales problems.

This kind of problem is a little surprising because logistics people are raised on the basics. Years of schooling and on-the-job training drive home the need to get the right product to the right place, at the right time, in the right condition. Why, then, do we see companies doing poorly in the basics?

The answer lies in the logistics culture of the organization--a culture largely created by management attitudes. Our research indicates the following are true: If management rewards logistics workers for **solving** the right detail problems, the logistics operation goes smoothly. On the other hand, if management penalizes logistics personnel for **creating or identifying** details that require attention, effectiveness wanes, regardless of how successful the logistics strategy.

A well-known foods company, for example, developed a superior logistics strategy (for attaining low-cost operations, proper service levels, etc.), and created an acceptable organization structure and a good customer-service orientation. Nevertheless, logistics' financial performance was not up to par with the firm's closest competitors. Return on logistics investment was only average, while the overall logistics cost exceeded 20 percent of the cost of sales. The economic value added by logistics was minimal. Fortunately, the company identified several gaps in the detailed implementation of its strategy and took steps to get the plan back on track. It revised operating performance reports to more effectively link strategy to operating performance measures and created "quality circles" at its plants to identify more effective operating procedures for adopting the strategy. In a matter of months, logistics' financial performance improved.

Getting back to basics in logistics need not be painful or dull. Nor does it require de-emphasizing strategy, planning, or other interesting management activities. What it demands is a refocusing of management and labor attitudes toward joint planning of tactics and strategy.

W. Edwards Deming writes, "Quality is everybody's job, but quality must be led by management."[13] Deming's 14 points for achieving and sustaining quality are as relevant to logistics operations as they are to manufacturing. They are as follows:

- Create constancy of purpose
- Adopt the new philosophy
- Cease dependence on mass inspection
- Stop awarding business on price tag only
- Continually improve the system
- Institute modern methods of training
- Institute modern methods of supervision
- Drive out fear

- Break down barriers between departments

- Eliminate numerical goals, slogans, etc.

- Eliminate work standards

- Give the worker his right to pride of workmanship

- Institute a vigorous program of education and retraining

- Create a management structure that pushes the 13 points every day

A back-to-basics focus underpins each of these points in the sense that doing the fundamentals right is what achieves quality over time. An important corollary is that understanding the fundamentals is key to doing them right. This is a company-wide effort. Senior management must communicate the strategic objectives and directions. Operations managers must provide the blueprint for change, figuring out the whys and hows of improvement. After all, the work force is only as good as the tools it uses.

In a book we wrote several years ago for the motor carrier industry--sponsored by the American Trucking Associations--we made the following observation:

> *"...The business of transporting freight represents a mature and established industry, and the basic services provided have been the same over the years. Essential changes in the marketing and delivery of these services, however, are required by today's environment...."*[14]

The same statement applies to logistics in general today. Its range of alternatives is greater and its potential for contributing to corporate profits virtually unlimited, but logistics' basic services remain the same. Innovation and creativity in logistics are important to competitive advantage. We found, however, that the attention to detail that leading companies provide for even the most basic services is equally important.

DOES SPECIALIZATION MANAGE THE DETAILS?

Frequently, in discussions of this manage-the-details principle, someone suggests the way to achieve it is to specialize. By having good, well-trained people in transportation, warehousing, order entry, administration, etc., a company can handle the basics. Again, this premise, although simplistic, contains some truth. Integrating these specialized talents to foster teamwork is essential. Isolated specialists tend to "build walls" that hamper a value-chain approach to operations.

During the last decade, Welch Foods created an integrated logistics operation incorporating purchasing, inventory management, customer service, transportation, and public warehousing. These functions originally operated as discrete cost centers, scattered throughout the company. The last element folded into logistics was purchasing--a move that gave logistics a comprehensive view of all materials flows.

Today, the Welch Foods director of logistics oversees all the above logistics activities, and reports to the senior vice president of operations. In essence, the company created a corporate department to manage all aspects of material flows on an integrated basis. At the same time, it set up specialists to oversee the specific functional areas of transportation, warehousing, and the like. These specialists manage the details. They also work as an integrated team to guarantee logistics performance.

What sets the Welch Foods logistics operation apart is management success at balancing the "large and small pictures" of its business. The company successfully created a department that controls total materials flows as well as details related to functions such as customer service, transportation, and warehousing.

Specialization does not guarantee detail management. Unless managed properly, specialization increases complexity and makes teamwork and activities coordination more difficult. Unless management recognizes and rewards effective detail handling, even the operations of the specialized function are not effective.

The Welch Foods approach to integration/specialization is not the norm. Business on the whole is moving toward greater specialization. We educate, train, organize, develop, and market with an increasingly narrow focus. In so specializing, we hope to concentrate resources, talent, and effort on specific operations, products, or services in order to become the best, be competitive, or to be efficient.

Professor Yoshi Tsurumi, a leading scholar and international expert (especially in United States-Japan relations), believes U.S. businesses are too specialized. In discussing logistics and overall corporate management, Dr. Tsurumi asserted to us that American firms--in contrast to Japanese companies that operate holistically--create rigidly segmented departments that foster corporate inflexibility. Also, too much specialization leads to sub-optimization of operations. In contrast, Japanese businesses focus on effective strategy and operations **simultaneously,** and so gain competitive advantage by setting strategies that the company is best equipped to implement.

To expand on this point, we cite **Made in Japan,** the autobiography of Aiko Morita, chairman of Sony Corporation.[15] Mr. Morita discusses how the traditional, multi-layered Japanese distribution system constrained Sony's new-product introductions and communications with consumers. To remedy this situation, Sony created new distribution channels. With the "Walkman" product, for instance, Sony built a sales and distribution network specifically for that merchandise. The company used the "old," multi-tiered distribution system where useful, but also set up its own wholesale and retail outlets and dealt directly with its dealers where possible. Under this set-up, Sony salesmen became "communicators," personally explaining product value and uses to those selling directly to consumers.

The Sony chairman goes on to describe how the company handled the complexity of marketing and distributing goods in the United States. Here too, Sony created new channels, including its own "showrooms." In the United States and elsewhere, Sony is careful to establish marketing and distribution systems that are compatible, yet innovative, with the host country. This typically involves working out a myriad of details that must be addressed locally.

Sony's distribution story bears out the fact that, even for a world-class corporation that manufactures outstanding products, a commitment to logistics and distribution must exist at the highest levels and extend to detailed operations. In addition, important logistics details should be considered at the very early stages of each new product, and existing distribution channels should be re-evaluated constantly. Failure to do so frustrates even the most innovative product and marketing plans.

MANAGING THE RIGHT STUFF

Knowing what details need attention, and keeping management on course in managing these details is a tough job--and the focus of our eighth principle of logistics excellence. Attention to random detail is not what this chapter is about.

To keep employees focused on "the right stuff," companies like General Motors Corporation and Ford Motor Company issue "management cards." These are glossy, pocket-sized cards on which the firms' guiding principles are printed. They serve as instant reminders of corporate goals. Ford prints its mission statement on its cards. That declaration took two years and hundreds of people to develop.

There are many distractions, alternatives, and opportunities available to managers today. Whatever a company can do to help its managers stay focused on objectives benefits the firm. Identifying the "right details"--i.e., those that are key to meeting strategic objectives--requires considerable management ability.

Referring again to the automotive sector, let's consider the logistics operations of Volvo Cars of North America. Volvo shares the industry's common goal of supplying a seemingly unlimited number of cars for immediate delivery. Simply put, it wants to "get the right car to the right place at the right time."

As an importer, Volvo faces special logistics challenges. It receives goods through 10 ports of entry, assembles cars in several plant locations, and distributes them to 480 dealers in North America. Through investment in improved planning and information systems, the company expects to shorten its order-to-delivery cycle significantly, thereby saving millions in inventory carrying costs, and boosting customer satisfaction.

The details-managing features of these new systems are two-fold. Volvo managers will get a software program that matches supply and demand at each dealership, and adjusts production plans at the earliest possible time. Managers also will have direct information links to dealers, districts, ports, auto carriers, and factories. Service, parts, finance, and other Volvo departments will share the common data generated via these links. In short, the company will manage every detail needed to control order and material flows. All parties in Volvo's operations chain will share these data.

Some logistics organizations use a technique called "benchmarking" to learn what details to manage. Benchmarking means a firm assesses the distribution operations of non-competing companies, and, where appropriate, applies what it learns to its own operations. Xerox Corporation is one of the pioneers in benchmarking. Xerox logistics executives used this innovative approach in converting the distribution function of Xerox's Business Systems Group from a cost center to a "simulated" profit center. A key element was comparing Xerox's operations with those of other, non-competing companies.[16]

Xerox first tried benchmarking in 1979. (Seymour Zivan, formerly vice president of logistics and distribution for the Xerox Business Systems Group, considers the technique one of the most effective methods available for improving logistics performance.) Prior to using benchmarking, the logistics function improved its productivity 3 to 5 percent each year--an unsatisfactory amount in light of industry-wide price cuts in business machines. Since using the benchmarking technique, the unit has boosted productivity 10 percent each year, and enjoys a better position against its competitors.

Most companies devote all their energies to learning what their direct competitors do in terms of logistics. Xerox does not, because management believes this approach creates problems. First, comparisons with competitors may uncover practices that are unworthy of emulation. Second, obtaining information from competitors is, of course, quite difficult. Although most companies "gather what they can" in market intelligence about competitors, little of real value can be learned from a non-cooperative source.

136

And third, Xerox believes its people are more receptive to new ideas that originate outside their industry. Although this last premise is debatable, it certainly works at Xerox.

Xerox logistics executives chose L.L. Bean as one of their first benchmark partners. As we noted earlier, L.L. Bean runs a highly regarded logistics operation. Its warehousing and order-service functions are particularly productive, reliable, and effective. L.L. Bean management agreed to work with Xerox on this project because the firms were not competitors, and because Bean managers believed they would benefit from the benchmarking process.

Over a period of several months, managers at the two companies compared operations, performance measures, work methods, and other logistics/distribution activities. As a result, Xerox incorporated some of L.L. Bean's practices into a warehousing modernization program. These practices included arranging materials location by velocity (to speed the flow of goods and minimize picker travel distance), and enhancing computer-based tools for picking operations. As we stated earlier, Xerox logistics reaped significant productivity improvements by applying its new-found knowledge. These 10 percent efficiency gains contribute directly to the company's bottom line.

THE BENEFITS? QUALITY AND CONSISTENCY

What are the major benefits of managing the details and how do the leading companies focus their efforts on the right details? A number of senior executives have told us that their companies use quality improvement to cut costs, increase productivity, and boost the bottom line. The quality they refer to is not restricted to product quality alone. Rather, their focus is on "quality in everything we do." Their measure of quality is compliance with their strategic plans and objectives--particularly the common goal of meeting customers' needs. Their approaches differ to reflect their industries, but all encompass four major cornerstones of an effective quality framework. These include:

- **Management commitment.** Meaningful quality improvement begins with probing senior management questions.

- **Employee involvement.** People and details are more important than indicators.

- **Appropriate use of technology.** Automation requires analyzing and restructuring the work process for simplicity and smooth, continuous flow.

- **Renewed emphasis on customers.** The company knows the benefit of a satisfied customer, versus the cost of a dissatisfied customer.

The goal of this approach is to ingrain a strategic focus and quality orientation in every employee. This goes well beyond worrying about "details" only when required to satisfy customer needs. It extends to the very "heart and soul" of the organization, as shown by one story we were told. It involved workers at a distribution center who had won a monetary award for the detailed operating improvements their quality circle team suggested. They used their award to buy a tree and a plaque. They planted the tree at the customer entrance to their distribution center.

The companies we have talked with are now leaders in quality, productivity, and profitability. But several attribute their success in part to making sure the "little things" are done right. As soon as these firms committed to improving quality, other problems disappeared. They reduced costs, eliminated errors, and improved product/service performance. These achievements, in turn, contributed positively to the firms' bottom lines.

Managing the details is not the only path to quality and profitability, of course. Without effective control of hourly, daily, or weekly "minor" problems, however, other efforts are wasted. When we see a smooth-running logistics operation in which the details are under control, we invariably find high-quality service and healthy profits.

Effective detail management also produces consistency. In today's companies, where multiple personnel, customers, departments, and disciplines interact across geographic regions, consistency can be a scarce commodity. Consistency of purpose, objectives, image, and information to customers--all are important. It is the logistics executive's job to manage the distribution process to ensure consistency. This means attending to the basics and rewarding employees for doing the right thing. It also means creating common procedures and functions to simplify the job of handling details.

Chapter 11
LEVERAGING LOGISTICS VOLUMES

For many organizations, logistics is a nationwide (or worldwide) activity that consumes millions of dollars in resources to effect critical linkages between the company, its customers, and its suppliers. However, that fact is well disguised when you review how some of these same companies manage their logistics operations. Their primary orientation is at the transaction level. They thoughtfully select the best carrier and routing of each shipment and assiduously verify the rating of each freight bill. As we describe in Chapter 10, attention to detail is **not** wrong. What is wrong, however, is a preoccupation with individual transactions and inadequate attention to managing major logistics flows.

Many shippers can gain a better perspective on what constitutes a more balanced view by studying the actions of the leading carriers who serve them. We are witnessing the emergence of new integrated transportation companies that offer a blend of air, truck, rail, and ocean services. By studying their major traffic flows and "leveraging" their freight volumes in the marketplace, carriers such as Federal Express, United Parcel Service, Roadway Express, CSX, and the airlines profit and grow. These firms actively seek economies of scale. As their managers well know, such economies allow the business to capitalize on high volume levels and maintain efficiency, both of which multiply operating gains.

The same leveraging opportunities are available to manufacturers, merchandisers, and distributors. Once logistics managers pinpoint **total** volumes of transportation, inventory, orders, space, and other physical elements handled **throughout** their companies, they can creatively manage freight flows, storage, and, ultimately, profits.

This "total-volume" approach, while seemingly obvious, is not easily achieved, particularly in multi-divisional corporations where decentralized business units "do their own thing." Despite such roadblocks, the excellent logistics organizations we interviewed find ways to understand, manage, and leverage their business effectively. In the following pages, we describe and illustrate the principle of leveraging logistics volumes.

UNDERSTANDING VOLUMES--KNOWLEDGE IS POWER

In company after company, regardless of its particular logistics mission and organization, we find that distribution managers have a clear grasp of how much they paid for freight services last period, how much inventory was stored at company-owned warehouses during a given time period, and how many outbound shipments moved last quarter. Beyond these basics, however, these same managers consistently have less-than-adequate knowledge about factors that generate real leverage in materials handling and transportation, and with carriers, suppliers, customers, and markets.

To illustrate this deficiency, consider the following list of questions logistics managers might use to determine whether their understanding of one key area--inbound logistics--is adequate:

- What is the corporation's total volume of inbound shipments?

- How much of inbound freight is:

--Purchased off-shore?

--Bought centrally?

--Bought by separate departments?

--Moved by truck? Rail? Intermodal? Other?

--Moved by private fleet vs. common carrier?

- How much, if any, inbound traffic is consolidated?

- What percentage of inbound logistics cost is actually planned and controlled by the logistics department?

- How much (and what) materials move intra-company (i.e., plant to warehouse, warehouse to warehouse, etc.)?

- How much does management know about the total inbound material flows of the corporation by item, location, product, and time period?

These questions are indicative of the kinds of issues the logistics manager must explore to gain knowledge, and to use that knowledge for leverage. There is no substitute for having timely, comprehensive, and reliable logistics information about corporate-wide flows, inventories, orders, and other related activities.

LEVERAGING TRANSPORTATION: CONSOLIDATION AND OTHER MANAGEMENT METHODS

With the increasing emphasis over the past decade on physical distribution--the movement of finished goods from plant location to customer (outbound logistics)--the functions of inbound logistics (purchasing, transportation, receiving, storage, handling) have been largely ignored. Even in outbound distribution, many companies have not taken full advantage of opportunities such as freight consolidation (combining two or more shipments in order to reduce freight rates on high-volume movements).

The excellent logistics organizations, however, make a point of tapping consolidation opportunities on outbound and, more recently, inbound traffic. These consolidation programs often provide an excellent basis for structuring strategic alliances with their leading carriers. In this way they make the carriers key partners in the value chain (described in detail in Chapter 7).

Warner Lambert Company, a manufacturer of health care and consumer products, successfully practices inbound consolidation. Based on a thorough understanding of inbound volumes from specific vendors, the company's managers created a 14-day cycle schedule during which products are made by the vendors, consolidated, and delivered to a Warner Lambert plant. This program not only reduced transportation costs, it more than doubled inventory turns.

Freight consolidation opportunities abound. They include grouping multiple orders into a single container, balancing inbound/outbound flows with in-transit inventory storage, and participating in multiple-consignor shipments arranged by shippers' agents and associations, freight brokers, or other third parties. Many motor carriers now offer effective consolidation services, with assembly and distribution tariffs, and proportional line-haul costs.

Consolidation is not new. Freight forwarders have practiced the technique for years to achieve economies of scale. Retailers, also, are veteran consolidators, particularly when buying within a regional market where vendors are nearby and orders are somewhat predictable. Manufacturers, on the other hand, have been slow to adopt the practice for inbound shipments, because of inattention or over-concern on the part of purchasing managers with unit cost and materials supply.

Sometimes, a multi-divisional corporation will "take control" of transportation flows to help its operating divisions gain leverage. For example, Gould, Inc., the electronics conglomerate, set up a "corporate transportation committee" to work with plant managers in its five divisions across the country. The committee helped plant managers understand what volumes and carriers were being used. It also showed managers how to turn these volumes into leverage to negotiate national agreements for better rates and services from selected carriers. As a result, Gould and its operating units saved money and improved performance. These kinds of programs are increasingly common today.

We recognize that managing transportation consolidations may require crossing organizational lines--between purchasing and transportation for example. Such actions may threaten department personnel unused to a cooperative environment. Gaining and sustaining cooperation, therefore, may take time. (One company devoted over two years to discussion, seminars, etc., before launching a consolidation program.) Senior management can shorten this time by committing to the goal, and reinforcing the teamwork behavior that helps achieve it.

Shipment consolidation may not be cost effective for every company. Nevertheless, an understanding of transportation flows is essential. Companies, particularly merchandisers and retailers, that deal with frequent small deliveries from scattered vendors may find that currently favorable rates for LTL (less-than-truckload) service make it the more economical way to manage inbound transportation. Still, management can gain leverage from large LTL volumes by working with a few selected carriers to gain better control of the goods flow.

Under deregulation, increased availability of public (common carrier) and private (owned and operated by the manufacturer, merchandiser, or distributor) transportation has created new options for the logistics manager. Frito-Lay, the grocery-products giant, recently emphasized use of its private fleet of 700 tractors and 1,700 trailers (key resources for its finished-goods delivery strategy) to haul more of its inbound freight for its 40 plants. The company carefully balances inbound and outbound movements to maximize its investment in highway equipment. Using a specially designed computer system, logistics managers schedule supplier pickups, coordinate backhauls with outbound deliveries, and pre-determine each pickup's weight and cube utilization, all based on plant production schedules. Is it any wonder that Frito-Lay is among the leaders in logistics effectiveness?

Regardless of the diverse methods companies use to leverage transportation volumes, one technique is common to all. This is the use of a routing guide, often touted as the "single most significant step taken to control transportation costs." A carefully planned guide helps manage the company's shipments efficiently and cost effectively.

Our research for this book revealed that the best logistics organizations follow a few basic principles in setting up and maintaining their shipment routing guides. First, they know their customers and preferred carriers very well. They are familiar with customer needs and preferences. They also understand their carriers' strengths and weaknesses, costs, facilities, and ability to provide extra services when needed. Second, they route their traffic to fit the carriers' service territories and rates. And third, they use their freight volumes as bargaining chips in negotiating attractive rates and services.

By observing these three rules, the best companies enforce and monitor their routing guide instructions. They work with their vendors and carriers to achieve smooth and efficient flows. In doing so, they save between 10 and 25 percent on transportation costs. At the larger corporations, these savings percentages amount to millions of dollars.

MATERIALS HANDLING--ANOTHER SOURCE OF LEVERAGE

Most discussions of gaining leverage from logistics focus on transportation volumes as the only area of potential savings. This narrow focus ignores a largely untapped sector of opportunity--materials handling. Admittedly, the growing emphasis on productivity improvement has focused management's attention on work-in-process inventories, parts handling, and other materials-storage and handling activities. In most cases, however, companies fail to exploit the volumes of materials available in the company.

Every manufacturing or distribution company has some kind of materials-handling system. Few, however, have company-wide strategies for managing total materials flow, storage, and handling processes. Consequently, it is rare to see a streamlined materials flow, with no excessive inventory, supporting production and distribution effectively. It also is rare to find materials-handling systems planned within the context of factory and warehouse improvements such as automation.

An integrated approach to managing materials flow is scarce because many companies do not understand their materials volumes--i.e., the complete flow of materials and products through their network of facilities. As a result, they do not devise an overall materials-flow strategy. Thus, individual projects, such as an improvement in one area of a warehouse, seldom generate the maximum payback possible. In extreme cases, the project may be shelved for lack of results. On the other hand, a materials-management system integrated into the full operations process produces tangible benefits of smooth materials flow. It helps reduce inventories and boost productivity.

Often, we see partial attempts to integrate materials flows into the whole manufacturing/distribution operation. For example, materials flow and production may be integrated, but support operations, such as warehousing and distribution storage and handling, are ignored. This kind of partial strategy may pare work-in-process inventories, but it does not address raw materials and finished-goods flows and volumes. It usually results from inadequate attention to several of the other principles of logistics excellence, and therein often lies the solution.

Inventory reduction can only go so far in cutting costs. Further savings must come from storage and retrieval systems that successfully balance the needs for fast access with the space economy. Automated storage and retrieval systems (AS/RS), in-plant transportation networks, overhead and workplace handling, and automatic identification techniques (bar-coding) represent opportunities for the future.

Companies that implement such materials-handling improvements reap remarkable gains in productivity, effectiveness, and contribution to profit. Frito-Lay, which is known for getting new products onto store shelves quickly and for filling orders with extreme accuracy (99.8 percent), recently opened highly automated warehousing and distribution facilities in California and Arizona. They provide:

- Automated control and tracking of inventory to produce timely shipments and ensure product freshness.

- Gentle, consistent handling to reduce breakage.

- Sufficient flexibility and expandability to guarantee good sales service and smooth new-product launches.

The operations integrate 12 automatic and manual operations and AS/RS systems that allow computer tracking of all materials (hundreds of line items). The systems provide real-time management of inventory and warehouse labor. They also direct forklift operators and provide dynamic product allocation capabilities to improve the company's ability to make last-minute operating changes. The facilities already are achieving higher productivity rates than other Frito-Lay centers, even in the areas of truck loading and palletization.

Many companies have similar automated distribution centers in various stages of planning, construction, or operation. What makes Frito-Lay's project noteworthy? Three points. First, it is an integrated production-warehousing-distribution operation. Second, it was designed as a total materials-management system, not an "islands-of-automation" project. And third, company management committed to the investment as a complete package because it addressed the full scope of present and future flow volumes. As testimony to the wisdom of management's decision, soon after opening, the Frito-Lay facility was shipping 30 percent more truckloads of product than in non-peak periods, without a hitch.

INTERNATIONAL LOGISTICS MANAGEMENT

For several years, we in logistics have been saying, "It's time to think international." Few would argue that we now do business in a "global" economy. It is increasingly difficult for a firm of any size to avoid involvement (or at least interest) in foreign or off-shore supply, production, or finished-goods distribution.

With international logistics, however, comes international problems-- problems of customs regulations, entry requirements, packaging standards, tariffs, currency translation, price controls, political constraints, and more. It may be years before these barriers are resolved sufficiently to permit smooth flow of goods across international borders. Until that time, companies that trade internationally must find ways to cope with such barriers. A number of our study participants have done just that--developed innovative logistics arrangements that set them apart from their competitors. These corporations use "logistics leverage" to create competitive advantage in world markets. Let's consider some examples.

One common way to gain international advantage is by entering into joint ventures and other types of strategic alliances. Proliferation of such alliances makes it more difficult to tell where a product is manufactured. For example, Mitsubishi makes Caterpillar equipment in Japan. IBM manufactures communications equipment for Nippon Telegraph and Telephone. In fact, U.S. and Japanese companies enter into dozens of cooperative business deals each year in industries such as steel, automobiles, computers, pharmaceuticals, telecommunications, and consumer electronics.

The business community likes these strategic alliances for several reasons, one of them being their physical distribution and product channel advantages. When companies mention logistics as a factor in establishing a strategic alliance, they often view their effort as a solution to a particular difficulty, e.g., the complex distribution system in Japan (or any foreign country, for that matter). In these instances, they see the foreign partner as the provider of "inside help."

For the world-class organizations in this study, however, this is not the only reason. Just as important to these executives is the ability to take advantage of their logistics volumes (suppliers or products) by entering into strategic alliances with companies that are expert in the host country at what they do--distributors, trading companies, or freight handlers, for example. The best logistics organizations secure alliances with the best companies to tap this expertise and to combine their volumes with those already flowing through well-established channels.

Toyota and General Motors, with their New United Motor Manufacturing, Inc. (NUMMI) operation in California (cited earlier in Chapter 7), have elevated the concept of the strategic alliance to a new level. Most of the publicity surrounding this venture focuses on the synergy of labor practices. GM logistics executives, however, are proud of the streamlined logistics pipeline created for the operation.

Specifically, NUMMI management operates with a focus on the whole logistics value chain, from materials supplier to end customer. (This concept is similar to the "demand-management" approach discussed in Chapter 5.) A satellite relays daily customer orders for new cars from the United States to a cluster of Toyota factories in Japan. Under a Just-in-Time fulfillment system, components are shipped as needed via containership between the various Japanese assembly plants and NUMMI. NUMMI executives established strict movement controls to eliminate container accumulation at the California plant. They also made their selected carriers and other vendors full partners in their logistics pipeline.

NUMMI's North American suppliers, about 75 at last count, are located throughout the continent. They receive weekly forecasts outlining seven weeks of shipping needs. Leaseway Transportation Corp. manages the domestic U.S. consolidation and delivery of parts from suppliers to NUMMI.

The Toyota-GM plant currently builds about 500 cars per day. The company constantly fine-tunes its logistics process, implementing many of the suggestions made by pipeline partners. At present, the entire car-manufacturing process--from order to delivery--takes under seven weeks.

By leveraging both Toyota's and GM's overall logistics volumes and expertise in Japan and the United States, NUMMI is achieving excellent logistics and manufacturing coordination on an international scale. Although the NUMMI example is somewhat unique in international logistics circles today, our research indicates that similar operations will become more commonplace in the near future. Our increasingly global economy, with points of supply, production, assembly, warehousing, and consumption located in different countries, will continue to challenge corporate and logistics executives to create more streamlined logistics systems. Managing total logistics volumes throughout the corporation, regardless of the business unit or product, will enable firms to establish arrangements that create international competitive advantage and avoid piecemeal operations that are disastrous for worldwide competitors.

LEVERAGING FOR THE FUTURE

During the past year or so, the concept of "third-party" or "contract" logistics has gained popularity in the United States. Already, it is a common practice in Europe, where manufacturing companies often contract with outside parties for services such as transportation, warehousing, and other distribution functions. The practice particularly appeals to those companies that view logistics as a necessary business expense rather than as a competitive weapon. This is not to suggest that contract logistics is simply a money-saving option. Outside service vendors, such as public warehouses, often can provide better, more cost-effective logistics service than the manufacturing firm.

Whether the logistics function is performed in-house or by an outside contractor, one fact remains clear. The practice of leveraging logistics volumes and flows will proliferate. Why? Because our increasingly global economy demands that companies constantly plan and evaluate logistics operations to stay competitive. Also, top management will continue to step up the pressure for logistics performance, especially return on assets.

As we explain in this chapter, excellent logistics departments strive to understand, measure, and monitor all logistics volumes that are ordered, transported, stored, and handled throughout the corporation as a whole. They collect this information for every product group from the entire logistics value chain--supplier to customer--regardless of organizational boundaries.

Once managers acquire this information, and ready access to it, opportunities to gain leverage or implement creative options will surface. Whether in freight consolidation, carrier or supplier management, inbound/outbound coordination, logistics investments, inventory turns, third-party support, or joint ventures, the ability to leverage logistics volumes will produce cost savings, improved profitability, and competitive advantage far into the future.

Chapter 12

MEASURING AND REACTING TO PERFORMANCE

At several points in this book, we have touched on the subject of establishing effective measures of logistics performance. Whether we talk about linking logistics strategy and operations to the corporate business strategy, focusing on financial performance, or measuring levels of customer service, all our principles of logistics excellence--at least in some measure--aim at understanding what is important to determining how well the logistics organization does its job.

In the preceding chapters, however, we did not elaborate on how the best logistics executives pay constant attention to measuring their units' performance, fine-tuning their measures, and responding to changing business conditions. Most companies realize that, in order to gain competitive advantage, they must improve their operations. Only the best, however, use their performance measurement systems to change their policies and priorities properly to sustain competitive advantage.

SUSTAINING LOGISTICS QUALITY

Top-quality performance, as we said earlier, means meeting customer requirements by doing the right things the right way the first time. Today, companies and their products or services have to earn a position of preferred status. Customers look for obvious merit or quality in products or services, otherwise they stop buying them. Many U.S. corporations have learned this lesson the hard way.

The logistics functions have just as large a role to play in sustaining quality as does manufacturing. We make this statement after observing world-class logistics organizations at companies such as IBM, Johnson & Johnson, Nabisco, General Motors, and Xerox. At each of these corporations, the quality performance of logistics people and service impresses customers as much as the products themselves. We do not mean that logistics could produce corporate success without quality products. However, we do find that, given a consistently good product, outstanding logistics performance adds real value to the business.

A prime illustration for this finding is the American textile industry. In recent years, this industry lost considerable market share to foreign competitors, despite the fact that it invested some $8.5 billion in new plants and processes. Moreover, the U.S. textile sector leads all others in productivity and quality. Many of these companies, however, have not given adequate attention to logistics and customer-service issues. If they had done more in these areas in the 1960s, perhaps they would not have given entree to foreign competitors.

One response to this predicament is for the textile manufacturers to complain, lobby for import controls, and cut costs dramatically (often killing their companies). If the industry already leads in productivity, though, where would more cost cuts come from? Another response is to capitalize at last on the natural logistics advantages U. S. textile manufacturers have over their foreign competitors. Some companies are taking this approach with some early success. The process is slow and arduous because, in part, it must overcome the very long lead times that have been traditional in the industry and that retailers have learned to accommodate. The quick order response capability some U. S. manufacturers are developing may be the key to their competitive advantage and, perhaps, to their very survival.

Because of its great promise, it is fast becoming an industry-wide initiative to developing an effective "quick-response" program. By implementing effective logistics practices, these domestic manufacturing and distribution operations deliver high-quality goods on time, with shorter lead times and faster order fills.

Clearly, a program like quick response must be sustained over time to have an impact. It also needs to be focused and fine-tuned to meet changing customer needs. Moreover, it must be measured in terms that customers relate to, and adjusted when new alternatives in transportation, order management, packaging, and other areas arise.

By calling the program quick response, and not Just-in-Time, the industry is creating a common identity and quality goal behind which all textile manufacturers and suppliers can rally. If the program's participants can sustain quality logistics and successfully exploit their location advantage, they may regain market share and enhance profitability.

BENCHMARKING: MEASURING LOGISTICS PERFORMANCE FOR ACTION

In order to continually improve an organization's effectiveness, management must uncover and adopt practices that improve performance on an ongoing basis. All too often, however, companies employ plans and monitoring methods that perpetuate the past. Technological and management breakthroughs go unnoticed, unused, or at best, recognized but not adopted.

As we mentioned in Chapter 10, one quality-related concept gaining popularity is benchmarking, or comparing one's business practices to "best industry practices." Generally, benchmarking is driven by the quest for quality improvement, or in the case of logistics, the desire to meet customer requirements in the most cost-effective manner. It focuses on individual "work groups" (such as a warehouse team) on the premise that quality begins and ends at the source, with people. The benchmarking process requires establishing recognition and reward systems to measure progress toward achieving strategic goals through individual and group objectives.

Again, as mentioned earlier, Xerox Corporation's Logistics and Distribution organization is a recognized leader in benchmarking. The company has for several years been updating its logistics and distribution organization under the corporation's "Innovation Renewal Program." Their incremental, building-block process is an excellent model of how to make steady evolutionary improvement--the approach clearly recommended by most executives we interviewed.

Initially, Xerox started its benchmarking program to give managers data about the performance and cost of Xerox functions compared with those of top competitors in each product market. The program was designed as the first major step in converting Xerox's logistics operation from a cost center to a functional profit center. Inherent in this conversion was the assumption that a distribution profit center must furnish service at competitive prices using inventory levels that its internal customers can afford to invest in.

The Xerox logistics managers used available industry data to create benchmarks for expenses, inventory turns, and associated levels of service. Data was gathered from three basic sources:

- Quotations from vendors for functions such as warehousing, truckload shipments, and packaging
- Companies with similar operations
- Companies in industries different from that of Xerox

Undergoing the benchmarking process yielded significant benefits to the Xerox logistics operation. The process produced:

- A clear organizational mission, goal, and success indicators
- Incentive systems with achievement rewards
- Active employee-involvement teams
- A clear set of identified customer needs
- A network redesign to reduce echelons and facilities
- Enhanced employee morale
- New and improved materials-handling systems
- Updated information systems
- Overall productivity improvements of 12 percent annually

Xerox executives define benchmarking as industrial research (rather than intelligence gathering) that allows a manager to compare his/her function's performance to the performance of the same function in other companies. Benchmarking is used to identify those management practices, processes, and methods the internal function group would have to employ if it existed in a competitive environment. Thus, it is an indicator of what a business function's performance "could be."

Because their emphasis is on identifying how current performance levels can be raised (rather than on what their competitors are doing), Xerox executives recommend that benchmarking be conducted with non-competing companies. Our research, however, reveals that three-fourths of those companies practicing benchmarking measure themselves against their competitors. While this is natural, because people want to be as good as or better than their rivals, it is not the best approach. It can stifle creativity, but more importantly the focus should be on competitive **differentiation**, not **replication**.

Further, obtaining good information about one's competitors is difficult. Consequently, companies that benchmark on competitors often do so at an aggregate level, measuring, for example, size of transportation expense, number of warehouses, and the like. This approach suffers from an excessive preoccupation with the query, "How are we doing vis-a-vis our competitors?" It hampers identification and analysis of how other companies are achieving their cost and service performance levels.

In addition, Xerox executives point out two other shortcomings in benchmarking against competitors. First, the process may uncover practices that are not excellent, and therefore not worthy of emulation. Second, while competitive benchmarking allows the company to match its competitors, it does not encourage creation of practices superior to those of rival companies. Taken together with the data-collection problem mentioned above, these drawbacks show competitive benchmarking as a risky and costly proposition.

The question then becomes, "How can we benchmark effectively against other companies that are in other product businesses?" Xerox managers pick out those companies, regardless of industry, that demonstrate superior performance in the functions to be benchmarked (e.g., transportation, warehousing, order processing). With the other company's cooperation their practices can be studied, documented, and assessed for their applicability. Management can then incorporate the best practices into its functions to work toward superior performance and competitive advantage. Indeed, Xerox found that their people are more receptive to new ideas and their creative adaptation when the ideas do not come from their own industry.

When benchmarking against non-competitors, logistics managers should follow several basic steps. They are as follows:

1. Identify what will be benchmarked. Xerox and other "winning" companies learned they cannot cover everything. Instead, they concentrate on those areas most critical to business success or on those activities causing the most trouble.

2. Decide who will do the benchmarking. Which employees should be selected to conduct the process? Probably a mix of line and staff concerned with the function(s) is the best solution, because of concerns for quality, continuity, and implementation of the adapted practices.

3. Determine which companies will be benchmarked. In discussing benchmarking, the question we hear most often is, "How do we select the benchmark companies?" Most managers are unfamiliar with companies outside their own industry. At the same time, they all want to study the "best" companies. What is best for one benchmarking, however, may not be the best for another. So, we need not find the "best" company in general; rather, we should look for excellence in the functions to be benchmarked. Published materials and communication networks, among other sources, can help identify candidates. Of course, candidates must be willing to participate in the project .

4. Perform the benchmark investigation. The benchmark team first must understand its function(s) completely; then it can visit other companies to compare and assess respective practices.

5. Validate improvement opportunities. Once the team has identified alternatives for improvement, it must relate these to customer requirements and impacts on strategic alliances and on other value chain partners. This helps ensure that the changes will truly yield the overall benefits sought.

6. Adopt the benchmarking results. Whether benchmarking spurs strategic redirection of the function, or a relatively minor adjustment to an operating method, executing changes takes much time and effort. Specific changes can be targeted in business or operating plans and communicated to management and the affected people. Milestones or other performance indicators should punctuate the implementation stage. Recognition points should be built into the learning curve.

One of Xerox's early experiences with benchmarking involved L. L. Bean. (We discussed L. L. Bean in earlier chapters, noting what makes this retailer a leader in certain logistics performance areas.) The Xerox/L.L. Bean project benefitted both organizations. Oriented toward warehouse productivity, the benchmark exercise identified dramatic differences in the respective performance factors for:

- Orders per person-day

- Lines per person-day

- Pieces per person-day

It also pinpointed differing approaches to materials handling.

Xerox managers adopted what they considered the "best" L.L. Bean practices for their operations. Xerox subsequently benchmarked against several other non-competitors and adapted other successful practices for its operations.

As a result of Xerox's continuous benchmarking process, and its selective and innovative application of "best practices," the company's logistics operations achieved remarkable gains in productivity and contributions to margins and profits. Clearly, Xerox's experience illustrates the benefits of benchmarking as a catalyst for **achieving** and **sustaining** logistics excellence.

One of the greatest benefits of the entire benchmarking process is its requirement for ongoing measurement of logistics performance. Benchmarking with other companies stimulates logistics managers to challenge the way their operations are measured, and to design new ways to measure performance. Such new performance measurements are critical to securing contribution to profit.

INTEGRATED LOGISTICS MANAGEMENT: ACTING ON PERFORMANCE MEASURES

Adopting effective performance measures is an important element in achieving logistics excellence, whether such measures are identified through benchmarking or more directly emanate from the company's own logistics plans and strategies. Even more important, however, is using those performance measures consistently to guide management action. The best logistics organizations attack this problem in two steps. First, they operate out of a unified and integrated logistics-management process linked directly to their overall logistics and business strategies. They then proceed to execute operations plans designed to achieve the levels of performance necessary to meet strategic objectives.

Let's elaborate on these points. With greater awareness of the importance of logistics to corporate profitability has come the realization that logistics functions must be managed in an integrated fashion. Returning to the value chain concept for a moment, we know that effective inbound logistics adds value to operations, which adds value to outbound logistics, which contributes to marketing, etc. Given this interconnectedness, obviously a company should manage its logistics pipeline as a whole.

As we discussed in Chapter 3, "Linking Logistics With Corporate Strategy," the distribution logistics system, with its network and operating rules, must function in support of the business goals. Establishing the right performance measures to monitor the degree of this support is a difficult job. An even tougher job, though, is deciding how to act on the basis of a performance problem or weakness.

With these difficulties in mind, we'll consider a few of the major indicators that call for change. Then we'll look at how the best logistics organizations correct their operations in response to these indicators.

Poor customer service. The most important goal of distribution is to serve the market. Any indication that service is inadequate or non-competitive suggests a need to re-evaluate the system. For example, companies may discern their service is poor through:

- An increasing frequency of customer complaints

- A survey of competitors' service levels

- Increasing frequency of stock-outs, back-orders, or emergency shipments

- Drop in sales, not due to price, product, or promotion

Poor customer service can arise from a number of causes, from basic or fundamental such as labor problems, to more complex or subtle, such as a divergence of logistics operating practices from sales and marketing initiatives resulting in frustration and customer dissatisfaction.

Corrective action often focuses narrowly on simplistic solutions, thereby overlooking the larger issues surrounding logistics strategy and integration. For example, one company we interviewed experienced stock-outs, back-orders, and emergency shipments because of weak logistics planning and integration with marketing and production. Dropping sales made corrective action necessary. Rather than look at ways to improve overall demand management, however, this company initially opted to increase inventory--the simplistic solution. Poor return-on-asset performance, however, quickly made management re-think its solution. The resulting integrated approach that was adopted improved customer service, restored sales levels, and reduced costs. Now detailed management focus is on its operations' strategic objectives, thereby minimizing the risk of getting out of sync with marketing and production in the future.

Excessive inventories. When it comes to inventory, there is no easy definition of "excessive." The following performance indicators, however, may signal a problem:

- An unfavorable comparison of turnovers with industry data

- A decline in turns as compared to previous periods

- An unfavorable analysis of returns generated by the increased investment in inventory levels

When performance measures indicate excessive inventories, managers again often focus on a relatively narrow cause such as changes in order patterns. Certainly, orders are the best measure of actual demand, but they may not pinpoint the real reason for the inventory problem. And, analysis of changed order patterns does not resolve the situation.

An integrated logistics approach, however, would examine the full value chain to assess whether changes in operations links are indicated. For example, production planning and market research may not coordinate their efforts. Thus, forecasts are not effectively translated into time-phased production.

Order-cycle time is another critical performance indicator, because it measures the lead time between order receipt and order shipment (and receipt by customers). Many firms get into difficulty because they measure only the mean time required to satisfy a customer's order, rather than the variances in each element of the order-fulfillment cycle. For example, a well-known grocery products company was relatively comfortable with its five-to-seven-day order lead time performance. When we analyzed each element of work comprising the lead time, however, we found that excessive checks and balances added as much as two days to the cycle. Simply by eliminating redundant controls, the company improved its competitive position--a subtle but significant change. This is an excellent example of managing details without understanding which details were important in achieving your strategic objectives.

A PERSPECTIVE ON LOGISTICS PERFORMANCE

We have suggested that corporations view logistics as a strategic tool rather than as a cost-incurring function, and that logistics coordinate its activities with production, sales, marketing, research and development, and other operating functions of the business. For logistics to perform in this manner, management must design its performance measures to monitor "how it is doing" in meeting the company's strategic goals. Additionally, logistics managers should be ready to take appropriate corrective action whenever logistics is not progressing appropriately toward achieving its strategic objectives.

When discussing performance measurement with logistics managers, we hear two common complaints. "Sure, we know **what** our logistics functions should be doing," these managers say, "but we just don't know how to get timely, reliable, and comprehensive information about **how well** we're doing." Or, these same executives comment, "We measure our operating performance pretty well, we think, but **our** measures are not meaningful for our **customers.**"

These two complaints embody the main thrust behind our principles of logistics excellence. They address two broad and essential goals: (1) positioning logistics within the corporate strategy so that it fully supports the business goals, and helps meet them profitably; and (2) focusing logistics on effective service to the firm's customers, in order to gain optimal profit from alternative service strategies.

The importance of measuring how well logistics meets these two challenges cannot be overstated. We recommend that logistics and other operating executives treat the measurement of logistics performance with the same care and attention they devote to measuring operations, systems, or personnel performance. This means the logistics executive should challenge existing measures, work to improve how performance is reported, and innovate, innovate, innovate. It also means the manager should focus on what the customers need, and how well the department meets those needs. Above all, a logistics executive should never accept yesterday's measures of performance as adequate for tomorrow.

PART III: CONCLUSIONS

Chapter 13

PUTTING IT ALL TOGETHER: WORLD-CLASS LOGISTICS AND PROFITS

Since 1985, when we began the research for this book, much has been written and done to address the "competitive crisis" besetting the U.S. industrial sector. Throughout the previous 12 chapters, we looked at some of the ills plaguing American competitiveness, and discussed ways in which the logistics function can make a difference to corporate profitability. We described innovative practices being executed within logistics organizations at several leading companies.

Is logistics innovation just another hopeful remedy? Do these innovative practices really give companies competitive advantage over their domestic and foreign competitors? Can achieving the 10 principles of logistics excellence really improve profitability?

Undoubtedly, readers of this book--or any manager seeking solutions to corporate problems or competitive threats--will ask these questions. Thus, in this final chapter, we will address these questions, and reflect on the context in which excellence in logistics--as **one** corporate function-- provides a measurable contribution to profitability (and, indeed, to survival). We offer this discussion with the full knowledge that improving logistics activities is **not** a panacea for corporate ills. Certainly in most companies, production (operations), sales and marketing, and service--the other three key value-added activities in a company's value chain--together represent substantially more resources and work processes and therefore can offer a combined greater impact on profitability than logistics. Nevertheless, logistics excellence can be an important weapon in the corporate competitive arsenal.

One of the intentions of this book is to raise top management's consciousness about the value of logistics to, as one CEO put it, "...improve my profits, to increase my share of the market, to improve my cash flow, to open new territories, to introduce new products...." We think the innovative logistics practices and their profit contributions described herein will capture the interest of many senior executives. We also hope that all business executives, regardless of their industry, will use this book to stimulate interest in capitalizing on logistics as a value-adding function.

In the preceding chapters, we described in detail the 10 principles of logistics excellence; we cited case examples of how certain executives have undertaken innovative practices that give life to these principles; we cited guidelines to help readers work toward improving practices in their companies; and we described the impact on profitability successful execution of the principles can achieve. The exhibit below lists the principles together. Can any company claim excellence in all 10 areas?

As we sum up our findings on logistics excellence in this chapter, we cannot sufficiently stress the fact that outstanding logistics performance can only be achieved by achieving and **sustaining** all 10 principles. The ability to sustain excellence is the true measure of a successful company. Instituting these principles can sustain long-term profitability, as opposed to short-term surges in the marketplace.

THE PRINCIPLES OF LOGISTICS EXCELLENCE

1 -- LINK LOGISTICS TO CORPORATE STRATEGY

2 -- ORGANIZE COMPREHENSIVELY

3 -- USE THE POWER OF INFORMATION

4 -- EMPHASIZE HUMAN RESOURCES

5 -- FORM STRATEGIC ALLIANCES

6 -- FOCUS ON FINANCIAL PERFORMANCE

7 -- TARGET OPTIMUM SERVICE LEVELS

8 -- MANAGE THE DETAILS

9 -- LEVERAGE LOGISTICS VOLUMES

10 -- MEASURE AND REACT TO PERFORMANCE

COMPETITIVENESS: SUCCEEDING IN MATURING MARKETS

In our discussions with senior executives in the course of this research, we detected widespread concern over penetration by foreign companies into domestic markets. Certainly almost every industry under the manufacturing umbrella has seen its earnings adversely affected by foreign competition.

These worries have escalated so dramatically that the U.S. Congress is considering legislative measures to protect certain American businesses from foreign competition. Although most industries feel the effects of off-shore competition, those most seriously impacted include:

- Aerospace and defense
- Apparel and textiles
- Construction
- Consumer products
- Energy
- High technology
- Telecommunications

To combat this competitive onslaught and bring the U.S. trade deficit down, the American manufacturing sector may have to grow by as much as 30 percent over the next five years, some economists believe. This is because our industrial competitiveness has slipped alarmingly in the past decade, and the country has become the world's leading debtor nation. Productivity has grown at less than one percent annually--a dangerously low figure.

The reasons, then, for committing to business excellence are clear. The difficulties lie in achieving that goal. To begin, American business must re-dedicate itself to unrelenting pursuit of the fundamentals that made us successful and competitive in the past. These key fundamentals include:

- New-product development
- Improved productivity

- Superior quality

- New technology

- Commitment to human resources

- Solid value offerings

- Aggressive sales and merchandising programs

- Effective product distribution and logistics

- Second-to-none customer service

These last two factors--distribution and logistics and customer service-- are what this book is about.

Regardless of its source--foreign or domestic--intensified competition is a fact of today's business life. All companies, therefore, should devote their energies and resources to understanding and prospering within their increasingly competitive markets.

Robert Fox, former chairman of Del Monte Corporation and a senior executive at RJR Nabisco, discussed this theme effectively.[17] In the following paragraphs, we incorporate many of Mr. Fox's thoughts. We consider the issues and principles discussed **directly** relevant to what most U.S. companies must do to compete in the 1990s.

Good products and sales, while still essential, are not enough. Companies must emphasize "total business management," and develop the ability to approach products, costs, markets, and even volume more critically than in the past. And they must develop a concise strategy to conduct it over time.

Today, the traditional product lines of most companies are firmly positioned. The challenge is to manage the business properly, to turn these core businesses into solid assets, earning a respectable return on the investments they represent.

The first step in achieving and sustaining profitability and competitive leverage is to recognize that managing a mature market is not the same as managing a growth market. The difference stems from the following four basic conditions of mature markets:

1) The rapid growth a mature market may have enjoyed in its formative years is almost certainly over, and efforts to sustain that growth will largely be unproductive.

2) The fact that mature industries are no longer growing does not mean they don't change. Technologies, production methods, packaging, distribution systems, and customer needs continue to evolve. In fact, studies show that innovation, especially in manufacturing, becomes more frequent as an industry matures and companies face greater competition.

3) Competition intensifies as a market matures. Corporate growth objectives often remain long after industry growth has slowed. Companies are fighting for a share of a pie that is growing more slowly, or even shrinking.

4) Attempts to meet intense competition head on in traditional ways, such as brand proliferation or heavy promotional activity, frequently are self-defeating. Even if increased production, inventory, and promotional costs capture additional volume, they also erode profitability. In a declining market, increased advertising budgets may help maintain share of market, but they seldom succeed in reversing a downward trend.

These conditions demand that management adopt certain key strategies--all of which relate to logistics and corporate profitability. These strategies are explained below.

Establish profit-oriented objectives. The first step is to establish clear objectives, taking care **not** to base them on absolute growth in volume or earnings. In a mature market, executives should not be pressured to pursue high-growth objectives or seek volume for volume's sake. Instead, their performance should be measured by how well they do in improving share of market, profitability, and return on assets or investment.

Companies seeking profitability in mature markets cannot overlook any means to create profitability--be it by reducing costs, volume, or assets, or increasing prices. The traditional approaches, such as elimination of excess inventory, are keys to improved returns. But if a company can manage its inventory on a permanent basis, the improvement can be lasting.

Take advantage of existing strengths. A mature company in a mature industry has probably been around for some time. No matter how much its profitability has eroded in recent years, it undoubtedly has strengths that younger competitors cannot match. Often, such strengths are present in a firm's most mature products.

Identify and exploit growth segments. Growth segments exist within every mature market. Forty years ago most advertising campaigns targeted the general public. Today, consumers are segmented into scores of buyer groups on the basis of age, background, geography, and life styles. The profitable company of the future will successfully identify and exploit specialized segments within its overall market.

Invest heavily in all phases of research. There is a definite correlation in mature sectors between increased research and development expenditures, and product improvement and return on investment. (This is not necessarily the case in growth markets.)

To identify growth segments, customer needs, and product opportunities, companies must conduct in-depth market and consumer research. The low success rate for new products proves that winning ideas are not obvious on the basis of intuition--even to companies with long experience. Indeed, old-line firms especially should guard against a temptation to skimp on consumer research.

Developing innovative, superior, differentiated products to meet specific consumer needs requires knowing customer requirements better than competitors. "Innovative," "superior," and "differentiated" are key words. The intense competition characterizing a mature market is more likely to exhaust a company's resources than increase its profitability, unless the firm can offer customers a unique, superior product that is both difficult and expensive for competitors to imitate. Effective research will also yield improvements in work methods and processes. Improvements in managing materials, managing demand, and acquiring equipment also yield profit contributions.

Emphasize real quality. Within mature industries we see a definite correlation between high product quality and high return on investment. To gain the edge in competitive mature markets, a manufacturer must offer customers a better product at lower cost of bringing it to market. The retail packaged grocery-product market clearly illustrates this premise. It has been estimated that the average brand-name food costs about 15 percent more than the average private-label item, and about 30 percent more than the generic product. With such a price gap, the brand-name producer must rely on higher quality to attract the buyer.

We have more to say on logistics quality of service later in this chapter. Quality has to be much more than a slogan; it must be institutionalized within the organization to really yield improvements. Performance, productivity, and return on assets, to name a few key measures, will only occur when true quality is sustained throughout the company.

Eliminate "dead wood." This can be one of the hardest decisions for an old-line company to make. Many firms take pride in the fact that they offer the broadest line of products nationally. Management, however, must recognize that this position today costs more than it earns. Companies need to discontinue those products that can't achieve desired levels of volume and profitability. Although these items may not be clear failures, neither are they clear winners. Companies must constantly challenge what they produce as well as how they produce it.

Reduce costs. Producers in mature markets have to trim costs--not just once, but continuously, in every area of the company. A mature company can tap organization-wide experience for ideas on cutting costs in materials, production, distribution, and marketing. At the same time, it should explore the value of investments in new, cost-saving methods and machinery.

Consolidations provide further opportunities for meaningful cost savings. Approached on a broad-enough scale--e.g., closing the least-efficient operations to free capital, equipment, and personnel to strengthen the most efficient--this strategy alone can improve return on investment (or assets). Profitability in mature, highly competitive markets demands the elimination of all waste and unessential overhead.

Develop effective managers. The corporation in mature sectors must develop effective management in every area of operation. It needs to nurture and support its managers as carefully as its products. It also should position managers carefully, recognizing that different market segments may require different management skills. A company will have a better chance of revitalizing a mature market if its employees regard their positions as attractive assignments, with as much potential for advancement as any other job.

In recent years, we have tended to equate maturity in the market with dullness and stagnation, as opposed to the excitement of growth products. The time has come for companies to revitalize positions in their mature businesses, where the possibility of earning worthwhile profits may be just as great, and the challenge of earning them even greater.

These strategies for competing in today's markets tie in nicely with the principles on striving for logistics excellence. In meeting the objectives reflected in the 10 principles of logistics excellence, companies will be well on their way toward implementing "total business management." A world-class logistics function, because of its positive interrelationship with virtually every corporate activity, can stimulate the kinds of tangible, operations-based improvements that can make the difference in competing in mature markets.

ONE BROAD SOLUTION: MORE COST-EFFECTIVE WAYS TO REACH PRESENT AND POTENTIAL CUSTOMERS

As another look at putting it all together, let's consider the effectiveness of distribution channels in reaching customers. Earlier in this book, we discussed the issues and challenges inherent in "re-thinking the company's distribution channels."[18] Choosing the right kinds of distribution channels and customer contact methods is a complex and crucial decision for most firms. There are more distribution options than ever, all of which can impact a company's business. Unless these choices are evaluated on a regular basis, competitors can create innovative distribution channels and grab market share before the company realizes it.

In evaluating distribution channels, virtually all the 10 principles of logistics excellence come into play. Indeed, almost all the innovative methods we discuss--from EDI to targeted customer service--can and should be evaluated in the context of improving how the firm disseminates its products. After all, proper contact and delivery of the order to the customer produces the sales revenue.

In evaluating its distribution channels, a company may ask the following questions:

- Are we using the most efficient channels of distribution?

- Do our distributors have enough technical know-how to sell newer, more complex products?

- Are our customers beginning to think of our product as a commodity? If so, should we put more emphasis on selling through distributors, and less on direct selling?

- Should we reorganize the sales force to make better use of salespeople's time?

- How can we use computers to back up our salespeople and distributors?

- Does telemarketing make sense for our company?

- Should we use computer-to-computer ordering?

More and more executives are asking these kinds of questions about their present distribution channels. They are doing so partly because of competitive pressures, partly because of transportation deregulation, and partly because of cost, quality, and effectiveness concerns.

Generally, manufacturers and merchandisers have three options for reaching prospects and customers. They may sell directly through their own company channels. Or, they can market through indirect channels, or employ supplementary methods of contact. Most firms now use a variety of channels.

The primary method of direct contact is through the corporation's field sales force, which may include both generalists and specialists. Generalists sell the company's product line to all kinds of customers. Specialists, as the word implies, cover only part of the market. For example, they may deal only with large-volume customers, with certain products in the company's line, with a particular industry, or with a particular type of distributor.

Companies often reach their prospects and customers indirectly through resellers. These are middlemen--typically industrial distributors, wholesalers, or independent retailers--who buy products from the manufacturer and sell them to end users. (A few firms maintain company-owned wholesale or retail outlets.) These resellers often are referred to as distributors.

Beyond these two channels, the most important contact methods are telemarketing, computer-to-computer ordering, and catalogs.

Costs are normally the driving force behind changes in distribution channels. Companies are increasingly aware of the economic costs of getting their products from the plant to the customer. These economic costs are not simply current out-of-pocket expenses. For example, the economic cost of inventory includes the cost of the capital tied up in the product (money that might be used more profitably elsewhere), and the cost of storing and insuring the materials and finished products. Most corporations do not charge their divisions for the use of that capital. A few, however, are beginning to.

Many end users are demanding that the supplies or components they purchase be delivered on a specific day, at a specific time. This practice reduces the costs of storing and handling items destined for use in their manufacturing processes. End users also are reducing their supplier base, giving their business to a few stable, reliable sources of supply.

Just-in-time production techniques are gaining popularity in the United States. Few manufacturers, however, are equipped to make Just-in-Time deliveries to customers all over the country. For that reason, the firms supplying components to JIT-based customers will grow more dependent on those distributors that are especially proficient at managing their warehouse and transportation operations. Companies that lead the way in forming these closer channel alliances will be better positioned to compete. On this issue, one executive told us, "If manufacturers develop loyal partnerships with distributors in this country, they probably can hold off or neutralize foreign competition. I'm not sure a lot of companies appreciate that, but it's a very viable defense."

The use of indirect selling outlets, i.e., distributors or independent retailers or wholesalers, seems to be growing in virtually every kind of market. At the same time, manufacturing and merchandising salespeople are moving toward specialization. They are spending less time selling their products, and more time giving technical advice and solving problems. Most companies today employ sales generalists and specialists. In coming years, however, many of these firms expect to become more dependent on specialists.

The distribution of a product may shift from one type of channel to another during the item's life cycle. When the product is first introduced, selling costs are likely to be high, partly because most of the selling is done by a technically trained, direct sales force. As the product becomes more established, the resellers can assume much of the selling job. That frees the direct salesperson to provide technical advice to large-volume purchasers or to those with more complex application problems.

A company may fine-tune its distribution channels by using one type of distributor in the product's early life cycle, and a different type in later stages. For instance, a manufacturer could start out by using distributors equipped to perform market-development work. These distributors locate potential prospects, show them how to use the product, and provide most of the services needed to support the item.

Later on, the company may shift to using a network of distributors who simply service accounts. These distributors do not spend any time looking for new customers; they simply stock the product and sell to present customers.

By adjusting a product's distribution channel system as the product ages, companies can reap significant cost savings. Only a few firms take advantage of these opportunities, however. Some wait until their products are well into middle age before shifting to less-costly distribution channels. As companies achieve better understanding of the full supply-demand chain, more companies will work with their partners to restructure product channel mixes more appropriately for their customer markets.

In a related development, we see executives concentrating attention less on their products, and more on their customers. These managers are defining their businesses in terms of customers' needs which, in turn, affect the company's choices of distribution channels.

Management at older companies once heavily dependent on direct selling may question the distributors' ability to perform **value-added** services in addition to supplying lower-cost distribution. Other firms may find it hard to treat the distributor as a partner. In some industries, manufacturers traditionally paid distributors little more than a survival margin. That practice is disappearing as more firms recognize the importance of a strong distributor network. Distributors, for their part, are more experienced in dealing with technology, finance, and marketing, all of which can generate capital for expanded operations.

Certainly, our principle of forming strategic alliances applies to company-distributor partnerships.

In re-thinking the company's distribution channels, we believe the key focus should be on customers and their needs. These needs may take the form of requirements for on-time delivery, undamaged and complete deliveries, correct billing, and continuous communications. More generally, customers may say they simply want "to buy, receive, and pay for products without a hassle." In many cases, the less-tangible aspects of the distribution channel--i.e., how customers are contacted and treated--determine whether customers buy.

ADVANCING TOWARD LOGISTICS EXCELLENCE: THE QUALITY-IMPROVEMENT PROCESS[19]

The turmoil in corporate America is forcing our business leaders to undertake the most radical reassessment of their practices since the end of World War II. Out of this soul-searching a new orientation is emerging--a focus on quality improvement with an eye toward managing the process of change.

David Kearns, chairman of Xerox Corporation, and the individual credited with leading the come-back of the company, once observed, "Most of us running major companies may not yet understand how much we will have to do differently to be successful."[20] Xerox changed its entire corporate focus and approach to business in its struggle to survive. It changed from a large organization where people derived satisfaction by looking at the next job rather than concentrating on their present work; where responsibility for making decisions was heavily centralized; and where emulating practices of the past was the rewarded corporate behavior.

To bring discipline to the company, Xerox executives instituted the strategy called "Leadership Through Quality" that employs many of the principles of excellence we describe in this book. "Leadership Through Quality" does not just mandate competitive analysis at all levels in the company. It also requires comparison of Xerox functional capabilities with those of leading firms identified by competitive analysis. All corporate functions must use the benchmarking technique to evaluate their success in meeting customer requirements at a level greater than, or at least commensurate with, the levels achieved by other firms. Through benchmarking, Xerox has been able to:

- Identify strategic directions.

- Quantify the opportunities available to Xerox (i.e., the size of the gap between what exists at Xerox and what could be accomplished under new strategic direction).

- Motivate all employees to seek out the best practices in any industry.

- Help overcome employee resistance to change.

As a part of the Leadership Through Quality strategy, Xerox created a system of employee rewards (usually monetary) and recognition (acknowledgment and appreciation) to motivate people to embrace change. Management rewards teamwork to eliminate destructive internal competition; it encourages employee involvement; and it has instituted benchmarking as an ongoing process at all levels.

At Xerox, corporate, business unit, and functional managers use benchmarking to establish performance goals for the company and its component parts. These goals represent responses to identified shortcomings in the organization's performance--shortcomings that must be corrected by effective change. For example, benchmarking against competitors may reveal that other firms are more profitable, have a higher return on assets, or a higher market share than Xerox. Benchmarking against non-competitors can show that, although the company is the industry's best practitioner of a specific function, it could improve by adopting practices used by these non-competing companies.

The logistics organization at Xerox participated in, and in some ways led, the Xerox turnaround. It produced amazing gains in productivity which, in turn, created appreciable contributions to profit.

Basically, the question addressed at Xerox was, "How can the logistics executive ensure that changes needed to maximize return on assets actually take place?" This meant resolving three issues:

- How does change within the logistics organization influence return on assets?

- How do you know of potential changes that could favorably affect return on assets?

- How do you motivate logistics people to seek out and implement needed changes?

In planning how to respond to these questions, logistics executives applied the "Quality Improvement Process." This concept, based on Leadership Through Quality, reaffirmed that the degree of profitability quality creates is the ultimate measure of success. The quality improvement process aimed to cut logistics' "cost of quality," including reducing the amount of business lost through poor quality.

Xerox executives define quality as **meeting customer requirements**. We can best understand this customer focus in the context of the change-management process at Xerox. To remain competitive, corporations constantly must improve their performance through changes in business practices. Some businesses may change their product or customer services;

others change customers, distribution systems, raw-materials procurement, or employee-reward practices.

But real improvements are difficult to make. Larger corporations may not operate under a process that identifies all opportunities for improvement. Often, management is satisfied with current bottom-line performance, so does not seek opportunities to improve the long-term picture. Without an effective quality improvement process, these companies seldom break through the status quo.

As we observed, most firms equate success with favorable current bottom-line results or performance to plan, not with performance that achieves longer-range objectives. Management is easily lulled by short-run results (performance to budget, stock price) and may miss underlying trends that warn of trouble. Consequently, the company fails to foresee an impending downturn, and is caught unprepared. The cost of having no quality improvement process is corporate stagnation--an environment that opens the door to competitors' assaults. Ultimately, these competitors will wrest market dominance from the stagnated company.

In focused discussions with Seymour Zivan, who at the time was Vice President of Logistics for Xerox--and he held this position from 1977 to 1987--we learned that Logistics and Distribution (L&D) at Xerox Corporation was responsible for distribution of equipment, service parts, and supplies in the United States. In addition to managing outbound flows, it was also responsible for inventory management and control of service parts and supplies. The department places orders for all parts and supplies; receives, packages, and warehouses these items; and manages the network that moves them along with equipment to the point of consumption.

L&D was part of the Business Systems Group (BSG), which is the marketing arm of Xerox in the United States. In 1986, L&D had 1,200 employees, managed over 70,000 stockkeeping units in parts inventories alone, and had an annual budget of approximately $200 million. Before, L&D existed without quantified customer requirements, and its services were provided at no cost to its customers. It operated at "low-risk," which meant it had high inventories, high expenses, and a high rate of emergency orders.

180

To guide the turnaround process for the organization, L&D managers adopted a number of basic planning principles, as follows:

- Provide competitive levels of service by market segment.

- Reduce unit costs.

- Increase inventory turns.

- Decrease number of echelons:

  -- Find the shortest path from source to use/consumption

  -- Handle material the least number of times.

- Decrease number of locations at an echelon.

- Centralize slow-moving and scheduled delivery material.

- Modernize facilities to state of the art:

  -- Materials-handling equipment

  --Control systems based on bar-code scanning data capture.

- Capitalize on opportunities presented by deregulated transportation.

- Examine where and how much packaging and labeling are essential to move material without damage.

- Deliver to customers unconstrained by arbitrary geographic or systems constraints.

- Provide all customers (external and internal) with services that fully satisfy their requirements.

- Postpone configuring systems until customer-specified order is received.

- Provide incentives for over-achieving through pre-planned recognition and reward systems.

Xerox's L&D managers applied the Quality Improvement Process (QIP) mentioned above to manage change, execute their departmental mission, and achieve the planning principles. This process is diagrammed below. Each of the three steps in the QIP process is designed to answer a series of questions (listed subsequently under their respective headings). The QIP was applied at every level of the L&D organization at Xerox. The results have been significant.

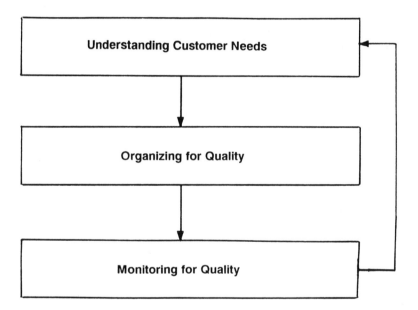

The Quality Improvement Process

UNDERSTANDING CUSTOMER NEEDS

-- Knowing what you do; who you do it for; and what their requirements are.

- What are the outputs you and your organization produce?

- Who is the customer (internal or external to the firm) for each output?

- Has the customer specified requirements for each output?

- Have you negotiated level of service and level of expense with each customer?

- Does your customer compare your effectiveness in producing each output with a "competitor"?

- Have you developed long-range targets for level of service, expenses, and assets based on benchmarking the best industry performers? Has your customer done this?

ORGANIZING FOR QUALITY

-- Identifying work processes and performance measures; adopting the right benchmarked methods; and recognizing and rewarding the right changes.

- Do you understand the work process steps employed to produce each output?

- Do you measure your success in meeting customer requirements in terms understood by your customer?

- Have you benchmarked your work process against others inside your firm, outside competitors, and non-competitors?

- Have you implemented improved processes learned from the benchmarking?

- Do your customers have the freedom to choose you as a vendor, or must they choose you?

MONITORING FOR QUALITY

-- Producing results; measuring work; and recognizing and rewarding improved performance.

- Does your new process really meet customer requirements?

- Have you reduced the cost of quality?

  -- Failure

  -- Locating failure

  -- Correcting failure

  -- Exceeding requirements

  -- Losing business

- Is the work process meeting requirements all the time? Is the process under control?

- Have you eliminated outputs for which there are no apparent customers? Outputs not performed in benchmark firms?

- Are your people recognized and rewarded when they achieve quality?

Over certain time periods, the results included:

- A 12 percent improvement in the expense/revenue ratio (4 years)
- A 29 percent improvement in inventory turn (4 years)
- A 20 percent reduction in emergency orders (6 months)
- Overall improvements in L&D return on assets

Through the QIP, L&D managers defined their work outputs, identified customers, and pinpointed their requirements. They compared the existing work process to industry benchmarks, and planned and implemented changes that transformed the work process to that benchmarked. Lastly, they recognized and rewarded these actions and their results.

This actual case example--taken from one of America's best-known corporations--serves to illustrate very well how a company can "pull it all together" to improve profitability.

To advance something significant like the Quality Improvement Process at Xerox, companies must combine methods such as benchmarking with positive reinforcement for change. Xerox executives have developed a unique recognition and reward system whereby team rewards were offered for overall functional achievement of the current year's expense and inventory goals. In addition, individual awards are given for projects aimed at future improvements but covered in current-year expense. For example, the company rewards an individual for completing a benchmark study that creates targets for future improvements. At the same time, it acknowledges another employee for integrating new benchmark methods to ensure future performance improvements.

Managing change for quality is a never-ending process--one that quickly loses focus without the backing of strong leadership. And, because logistics and other managers have at their disposal huge amounts of information and an array of technology to capture, store, transmit, and review this information, successful improvements are reached only when following a systematic process such as the QIP. For an organization to improve its effectiveness, it must first uncover and adopt practices and processes that will actually improve performance. We find many companies using planning and recognition systems that lead them to emulate the past, while both technological and managerial breakthroughs go unnoticed and unused.

If we can identify, implement, and adjust a logistics (or any corporate function) system that improves performance, rather than rewarding past performance measures, we are well on the way to enhancing corporate profitability. The QIP is designed to do just that, by determining the needs of all customers who demand outputs. These customers may be either within or outside the company.

Once the process identifies the appropriate changes, they need to be adopted effectively within the logistics organization. This will only take place if logistics people have work objectives that are directed at improved performance. And they must be recognized and rewarded individually and group-wide for doing the right things.

The Xerox success story illustrates how companies can push toward logistics excellence, and use logistics to make a real contribution to profits. We offer the 10 principles of logistics excellence described in this book as goals for all companies. Progress toward achieving these goals can translate into true competitive advantage.

In both the current and future competitive business environment, we believe it inadequate for any company to develop and execute strategy that merely fulfills marketing plans at lowest total cost. Logistics holds an increasingly important place in the corporation today, interfacing with manufacturing, merchandising, sales and marketing, and service. The challenge facing companies today is to take full advantage of logistics as a powerful competitive weapon. By organizing, focusing, and advancing logistics to excellence, it will make its real contributions to corporate profitability.

NOTES

CHAPTER 1: THE ROLE OF LOGISTICS IN PROFITABLE COMPANIES

[1] Michael E. Porter. **Competitive Strategy: Techniques for Analyzing Industries and Competitors** (New York: Free Press, 1980), pp. 34-44.

[2] Michael E. Porter. **Competitive Advantage: Creating and Sustaining Superior Performance** (New York: Free Press, 1985).

[3] Thomas J. Peters and Robert H. Waterman, Jr. **In Search of Excellence: Lessons from America's Best-Run Companies** (New York: Warner Books, 1982).

CHAPTER 3: LINKING LOGISTICS TO CORPORATE STRATEGY

[4] Manufacturing Studies Board, Commission on Engineering and Technical Systems. **Toward a New Era in U.S. Manufacturing** (Washington, D.C., National Academy Press, October 1986), pp. 4-8.

[5] "The Quality Imperative," **Fortune** (New York: Time, Inc., September 29, 1986), Special Advertising Section.

CHAPTER 4: ORGANIZING COMPREHENSIVELY

[6] Bernard La Londe, John R. Grabner, Jr., and James F. Robeson. "Integrated Distribution Systems: Past, Present and Future," **The Distribution Handbook** (New York: Free Press, 1985), pp. 16-19.

[7] James C. Riviere. "An Image Program for Logistics Personnel," **Logistics: Change and Synthesis** (Logistics Resource Forum, Leaseway Transportation Corp., 1984), pp. 199-206.

CHAPTER 6: EMPHASIZING HUMAN RESOURCES

[8] Mark McCormack. **What They Don't Teach You At Harvard Business School** (Glasgow:Wm. Collins Sons & Co., Ltd., 1984), p. 21.

CHAPTER 7: FORMING STRATEGIC ALLIANCES

[9] E. J. Muller. "New United Motor Manufacturing, Inc. (NUMMI)," **Distribution** (Radnor, PA: Chilton Co., October 1986), pp. 53-60.

CHAPTER 8: FOCUSING ON FINANCIAL PERFORMANCE

[10] Our earlier research and books were also sponsored by The Council of Logistics Management and The National Association of Accountants.

CHAPTER 9: TARGETING OPTIMUM SERVICE LEVELS

[11] This concept has been published widely in logistics and customer service industry journals. We believe it was introduced, however, by Harvey N. Shycon (now with Ernst & Whinney) in his article in the **Harvard Business Review,** July-August 1975, called "Put a Price Tag on Your Customer Service Levels." Moreover, in the 1985-1986 "Presidential Issue" of **Handling & Shipping Management** he elaborated on it in, "Distribution Earns Esteem and Profits."

[12] This ten years of study was initiated by the **HBR** article cited above.

CHAPTER 10: MANAGING THE DETAILS

[13] See, for example, **Out of the Crisis,** by W. Edwards Deming, MIT Center for Advanced Engineering Study. Deming, of course, has published widely. Another of his remarkable quotes is ... "Who can put a price on a satisfied customer, and who can figure the cost of a dissatisfied customer...?" This quote was printed in **Fortune,** Special Advertising Section, "The Quality Imperative," September 29, 1986.

[14] Patrick M. Byrne and Gene Tyndall. **Effective Marketing for Motor Carriers: Planning for Improved Profitability** (Washington, D.C.: American Trucking Associations, 1984), pp. 12.

[15] Aiko Morita, E. Reingold, and M. Shimomur. **Made in Japan: Aiko Morita and Sony** (New York: E.P. Dutton, 1986), pp. 74-97.

[16] This program is referenced elsewhere in the report. See Chapter 13 for the full context of the Xerox success story.

CHAPTER 13: PUTTING IT ALL TOGETHER: WORLD-CLASS LOGISTICS AND PROFITS

[17] Robert A. Fox, "Competition in Mature Markets," a presentation to marketing managers in 1985.

[18] One especially interesting report in this area is "Re-thinking the Company's Selling and Distribution Channels," by Howard Sutton for The Conference Board, Inc., 1986.

[19] This section is derived from several sources: Frances Gaither Tucker and Seymour M. Zivan, "The Change Management Process," in **Managing Logistics Change Through Innovative Information Technology,** Joseph E. McKeon, Editor, Leaseway Transportation and The Ohio State University, 1986; Frances Gaither Tucker, Seymour M. Zivan, and Robert C. Camp, "How to Measure Yourself Against the Best," **Harvard Business Review,** Jan.-Feb., 1987; and from materials prepared by Seymour Zivan as Vice President at Xerox.

[20] "Remaking the American CEO," **The New York Times** (New York, January 25, 1987).